NAVIGATING NONLINEAR CAREERS

Embracing Your Unique Path to Success

KRISTIN JEMISON

Navigating Nonlinear Careers © Copyright 2024 Kristin Jemison

All rights reserved. No part of this publication may be reproduced, distributed or transmitted in any form or by any means, including photocopying, recording, or other electronic or mechanical methods, without the prior written permission of the publisher, except in the case of brief quotations embodied in critical reviews and certain other noncommercial uses permitted by copyright law.

Although the author and publisher have made every effort to ensure that the information in this book was correct at press time, the author and publisher do not assume and hereby disclaim any liability to any party for any loss, damage, or disruption caused by errors or omissions, whether such errors or omissions result from negligence, accident, or any other cause.

Adherence to all applicable laws and regulations, including international, federal, state and local governing professional licensing, business practices, advertising, and all other aspects of doing business in the US, Canada or any other jurisdiction is the sole responsibility of the reader and consumer.

Neither the author nor the publisher assumes any responsibility or liability whatsoever on behalf of the consumer or reader of this material. Any perceived slight of any individual or organization is purely unintentional.

The resources in this book are provided for informational purposes only and should not be used to replace the specialized training and professional judgment of a health care or mental health care professional.

Neither the author nor the publisher can be held responsible for the use of the information provided within this book. Please always consult a trained professional before making any decision regarding treatment of yourself or others.

For more information, email youremailhere@youremail.com.

ISBN: 979-8-89316-423-7 - eBook
ISBN: 979-8-89316-424-4 - Paperback

For the innovators, changemakers, and risk-takers—whether in the corporate world, on the frontlines of social change, or building a business from the ground up—your diverse experiences are the keys to your impact

TABLE OF CONTENTS

Introduction vii

Chapter 1. Create Space 1
Chapter 2. Know Thyself 9
Chapter 3. You Are a STAR 23
Chapter 4. Create Your Career Narrative 36
Chapter 5. Own It 52
Chapter 6. Feel It 59
Chapter 7. Communicate It 64
Chapter 8. The Power of Networking 76
Chapter 9. The Art of Receiving 92
Chapter 10. Position It 102

Conclusion: Embracing Your Nonlinear Career Path 117

INTRODUCTION

In today's rapidly evolving professional landscape, the notion of a linear career trajectory—one that follows a predictable path from entry-level to executive positions within a single company or industry—is becoming increasingly outdated. More and more professionals find themselves on a nonlinear career path, whether by choice or necessity, navigating a series of varied roles, industries, and responsibilities that don't fit the traditional mold. For many, this shift from the conventional to the unconventional is both daunting and liberating. A question then arises: How do you make sense of a nonlinear career, and more importantly, how do you create a career that not only makes sense but also fulfills you and plays to your unique strengths?

The problem facing many professionals today is the outdated expectation that success must be achieved through a straightforward, linear progression in one's career. This mindset is reinforced by societal norms, traditional corporate structures, and even our educational systems, which often prepare us for a single career track. When reality deviates from this expectation—due to industry disruptions, personal choices, or unforeseen circumstances—many people are left feeling lost, undervalued, or even ashamed of their diverse experiences. They might ask themselves, "Why can't I just stick to one thing?" or "Am I failing because my career doesn't look like everyone else's?" This disorientation is often compounded by the pervasive belief that specialization is the key to success. In a world that values niche expertise, those with broad experiences across multiple fields might feel like they don't fit anywhere, leading to a lack of confidence and difficulty in articulating their unique value to potential employers or business partners.

The solution lies in embracing your nonlinear career path as a powerful asset rather than a liability. This book is designed to guide you through the process of understanding, owning, and strategically leveraging your diverse career experiences to create a fulfilling professional life. Instead of viewing your varied roles and industries as a disjointed series of jobs, you'll learn to craft a cohesive narrative that highlights your adaptability, resilience, and unique skill set. Through personal stories, practical exercises, and actionable advice, I will show you how to identify the common threads that run through your career, articulate your value proposition clearly, and position yourself as a versatile and innovative professional. This approach not only helps you build confidence but also opens doors to opportunities that align with your broader aspirations and values.

How I Can Help

My own career has been anything but linear, spanning multiple roles in the biopharmaceutical industry and including significant setbacks. I've experienced firsthand the challenges of navigating a nonlinear career path, from confusion and self-doubt to the ultimate realization that my diverse experiences are my greatest strength. For over twenty years I climbed the corporate ladder, only to be unexpectedly laid off after twenty-three years of service. This pivotal moment forced me to confront the reality of my career choices and ultimately led me to embrace my multifaceted professional identity. Instead of seeking another role that might confine me to a single path, I embarked on a journey of self-discovery, clarity, and ultimately, empowerment. My experiences, coupled with my commitment to continuous learning and personal growth, have equipped me with unique insights and strategies that I now share with you in this book.

What You Will Get
By reading this book, you'll

- gain the tools and insights needed to reframe your nonlinear career as a narrative of growth, learning, and adaptability
- learn to see your varied experiences not as a series of disconnected roles but as a rich tapestry that illustrates your ability to thrive in different environments, solve complex problems, and continuously evolve
- not only boost your confidence but also enable you to present yourself more compellingly in interviews, networking opportunities, and other professional settings
- be equipped with practical strategies to identify and articulate your unique value proposition (UVP), set clear career goals that align with your passions, and create a personal brand that reflects the full spectrum of your capabilities

Whether you're looking to pivot to a new industry, secure a promotion, or launch your own business, the insights and tools you'll gain here will empower you to take control of your career and achieve your goals on your terms.

Throughout the book, you'll find examples of frameworks that have been used by countless individuals, including myself, to successfully navigate nonlinear career paths and achieve remarkable success by embracing their unique journeys. Additionally, you'll find case studies demonstrating that a nonlinear career can lead to opportunities for innovation, leadership, and personal fulfillment that a traditional career path might not offer. From entrepreneurs who have turned diverse skill sets into thriving businesses to professionals who have transitioned between seemingly unrelated industries with ease, these stories will inspire and motivate you to see the possibilities within your own career.

By the end of this book, you will have the clarity, confidence, and actionable steps to create the nonlinear career of your dreams. You will no longer feel the need to apologize for or downplay your diverse experiences; instead, you will proudly own them as the powerful assets they are. You'll be equipped to craft a compelling narrative that positions you as a unique and valuable professional, capable of thriving in an ever-changing world. Whether your goal is to ascend to a leadership position, switch industries, or start your own venture, this book will guide you on the path to success.

If you're waiting for the perfect moment to take control of your career, there's no better time than now. The longer you wait, the more opportunities you might miss and the more likely you are to remain stuck in a career that doesn't fulfill you. Don't let fear, doubt, or the opinions of others hold you back from pursuing the career you truly want. The tools and strategies in this book will help you overcome those barriers, but only if you take the initiative to apply them.

So are you ready to take the first step toward creating the nonlinear career of your dreams? If so, I invite you to dive into the chapters that follow with an open mind and a willingness to embrace your unique journey. This book is your guide to transforming your career narrative, unlocking new opportunities, and achieving the professional fulfillment you deserve. Let's get started!

CHAPTER 1

CREATE SPACE

Silence is a source of great strength.
—*Lao Tzu*

I remember the exact moment I was laid off on Wednesday, July 12, 2023. I had a thirty-minute meeting added to my calendar by my one-up manager's executive assistant that morning. If you've been in a corporate setting for any length of time, you know the type of meeting I'm talking about—the one where you learn someone is either coming or going.

Since at the time I was leading a large external benchmarking initiative on behalf of the business unit, I assumed that the meeting was for us to align our thoughts on an upcoming readout with the consulting firm conducting activities on our behalf. After all, I was a twenty-three-year company veteran with an impressive list of accomplishments across several functions and business units. I had both performance and reputational credibility across the company. What else could it be about?

I continue to be grateful for the fact that I chose to work from home that day. As I entered the meeting virtually, I immediately felt tension and anxiety. No time was wasted getting to the point.

"Kristin, thanks for coming. Linda from HR is also here to support us through this conversation. As you are aware, the company has been reevaluating our organizational structure as part of our large enterprise initiative. Several areas of the business are being impacted and forced to reassess the way they work and operate, ours included. Over the past few months, we have been evaluating our organizational structure and . . ."

It was right about then that I realized this meeting was not about aligning on the agenda for an upcoming meeting. This was when I got the sinking feeling in my stomach, had the wave of fear come over me, and saw the words "I think I'm losing my job" flash through my mind like a message running across a digital signage board.

". . . as a result of these evaluations, I'm sorry to inform you your position is being eliminated."

I have a difficult time recalling the rest of the conversation that followed because I temporarily went into shock. I was tuned in enough to learn I would have a ninety-day transition period and that my last day would officially be October 12, 2023, unless I found another internal role by that time.

"Do you have any questions?"

Plenty—only one of which I felt would serve me moving forward and bring me peace: "Was this decision in any way based on my performance?"

"No."

Job loss is a profound event that can mirror or even surpass the trauma of losing a loved one. The psychological impact extends beyond financial implications, triggering a profound sense of grief akin to mourning a death, with stages such as denial, anger, bargaining, depression, and acceptance. This response stems from the fact that work often forms a core part of our identity, purpose, and daily routine, making its loss a significant personal blow.

Unlike the loss of a loved one, which garners sympathy and support, job loss can lead to feelings of shame, isolation, and a diminished sense of self-worth. These factors exacerbate the psychological toll, potentially resulting in conditions like anxiety, depression, and even PTSD. Moreover, job loss disrupts social structures and daily routines, contributing to feelings of disorientation and loss of purpose. The sudden cessation of work-related activities can leave a void in one's life.[1]

In the days and weeks that followed, I cycled through each of the five stages of grief, sometimes all within the same hour.

- *They made a mistake; they meant to call someone else into that meeting. (denial)*
- *After everything I've sacrificed for the company, this is how I'm treated?! (anger)*
- *If I hadn't been so outspoken, they might have chosen someone else. (bargaining)*
- *No one else will ever want to hire me. (depression)*
- *I'll be all right. (acceptance)*

For the first two weeks after I lost my job, I swore my husband to secrecy. I didn't tell anyone—not my parents, my closest friends, or my siblings. No one. I had been employed since I was sixteen years old. After thirty straight years of working, I found myself unemployed for the first time in my life. I felt humiliated. Embarrassed. Less than. I worried what others would think and how future employers would judge my potential gap in employment. Worse, I felt that a part of

---

[1] "The Toll of Job Loss on Mental Health," American Psychological Association, October 1, 2020, https://www.apa.org/monitor/2020/10/toll-job-loss; José Antonio Climent-Rodríguez et al., "Grieving for Job Loss and Its Relation to the Employability of Older Jobseekers," *Frontiers in Psychology* 10 (2019), https://doi.org/10.3389/fpsyg.2019.00366; Matthew P. Crayne, "The Traumatic Impact of Job Loss and Job Search in the Aftermath of COVID-19," *Psychological Trauma: Theory, Research, Practice, and Policy* 12, no. S1 (August 2020): S180–S182, ResearchGate.

my identity, one that had been a vital part of how I saw myself in the world, had been ripped away from me. What was I supposed to do now?

I kept going through the motions of getting up, going to the gym, showering, and driving in to the office because that's what I had been conditioned to do. I also still had a transition plan to execute and hopes of securing a new internal role in another business unit that I had interviewed for a month prior. On the outside, I kept up the facade of business as usual.

On the inside, I had absolutely no desire to work, look for a new job, or even try to generate the motivation I would need to sell myself to a prospective employer in an interview. I started thinking about whether I truly wanted the internal role I had interviewed for. Would it just be more of the same as the past three years—me feeling like I had more to give and not having the opportunity to do so? Would I ever be able to realize my full potential here?

By the beginning of August, all my responsibilities had been reassigned and I now had a lot of time on my hands. I was encouraged to use my remaining two and a half months with the company to do whatever I needed to do to find my next role.

I had no idea what to do with myself. My Outlook calendar had dictated my every move for the better part of the last fifteen years. Time scarcity used to be my biggest enemy, and now all I had was time. Anxiety and fear were my faithful companions every minute of the day. Each day that passed became a bit darker than the previous one, and I felt myself going to a place I feared I might not be able to pull myself out of. Desperate to move past those feelings and get the answers I sought about what my next career move should be, I moved from thought to thought. Do I stay or do I go? And if I go, where do I go and what do I do? What do I want to be in ten years? More anxiety.

One day, I was lethargically scrolling through Facebook when I came across an ad by a career coach. I was intrigued since enlisting the help of a career coach had been something I'd been putting off for years. At this point I had nothing to lose, so I clicked to receive the free masterclass. My interest grew enough after attending the class to book a clarity call. When the coach said they thought they could help me, I hemmed and hawed a bit at the price. I questioned if I was worth it, if I should be spending that kind of money on myself, having just lost my job. But I knew in my heart that I had lost myself and needed to claim myself again. I signed up on the spot.

Through my onboarding, I was introduced to a morning routine, strongly encouraged for all participants, of meditation, practicing gratitude, and journaling to bring my nervous system out of fight-or-flight mode and help me get back in touch with my soul. I had never formally meditated before, but at this point I was willing to try anything that might offer relief from the anxiety and angst I had been feeling for weeks. At first I had difficulty concentrating. I could barely sit still for more than a few minutes in a row. My mind wandered and became easily distracted. I became impatient, wondering if I was doing it "right" and judgmental of my not being able to quiet my mind. I would mentally yank my mind back, almost violently at first, giving myself no credit for trying something new and demonstrating little to no self-compassion

I have always prided myself on not being a quitter, and this was no different. Despite the difficulties I was having, I stayed the course. After a few days I began noticing subtle shifts in my meditation experiences: longer periods of focus, a greater ability to observe thoughts without getting lost in them, and a gradual sense of calmness or mindfulness that was extending into my daily life. Two minutes turned into five minutes, and five minutes soon turned into ten. I felt like I was on my way to a better version of me.

I found this routine to be extremely therapeutic. I created a space to pause, reflect, listen, and be guided by my soul for the first time ever. Within my first week of daily meditations, I received a clear-as-day message that I would never recognize my full potential at my current employer. I knew at that moment I would take the severance package and leave.

This clarity made me feel powerful. For the first time in a long time, I was in control of my life, no longer doing what everyone else thought I should do or accepting where others tried to steer my career. I was taking charge. I withdrew my candidacy for the internal role I had interviewed for as well as for another role for which I was progressing through the recruiting process. I informed everyone who asked that I was taking the package. While this decision was both empowering and frightening, for the first time in a long time, I was back in the driver's seat, steering the direction of my life rather than watching it from the passenger seat. There was something both terrifying and exciting about answering the question "What's next for you?" with an exhilarated "I don't know!"

A regular meditation practice can have many benefits. It can help cultivate a sense of inner peace and calm amid the chaos of daily life. By learning to observe our thoughts and emotions without judgment, we can develop a greater sense of equanimity and resilience in the face of stressors. You may find, like I did, that you can better navigate challenging situations with a sense of clarity and composure.

Meditation can have profound effects on emotional well-being. Through regular practice, I became more attuned to my emotions and was better able to regulate them. As the weeks and months went on, I experienced reduced levels of anxiety, depression, and other negative emotions, as well as an increase in positive emotions such as gratitude, compassion, and joy.

Establish a Personal Self-Care Routine

- **Set clear expectations:** Begin by clarifying why you want to establish a daily meditation and self-care routine. Reflect on the specific benefits you hope to experience, such as reduced stress, improved focus, or enhanced emotional well-being. Setting clear intentions will help you stay motivated and committed to your practice.

- **Start small:** It's essential to start small when building a new routine. Begin by allocating just a few minutes each day to meditation and self-care activities. Doing this makes the practice feel more manageable and increases your likelihood of sticking with it over the long term. Gradually increase the duration and complexity of your routine as you become more comfortable.
- **Choose a consistent time and space:** Select a specific time of day and a quiet, comfortable space where you can dedicate yourself to your meditation and self-care practice. Consistency is key to forming a habit, so try to meditate and engage in self-care activities at the same time and place each day. This helps signal to your mind and body that it's time to relax and recharge.
- **Experiment with different techniques:** Explore various meditation techniques and self-care practices to find what resonates best with you. These could include mindfulness meditation, guided visualization, deep breathing exercises, journaling, gentle stretching, or spending time in nature. Be open-minded and willing to experiment until you discover what feels most nourishing and fulfilling for you.
- **Stay accountable:** Hold yourself accountable to your daily meditation and self-care routine by tracking your progress and celebrating your successes. You can use a journal or habit-tracking app to monitor your consistency and reflect on how the practice is impacting your well-being. Additionally, consider sharing your goals and progress with a supportive friend or joining a meditation group or online community for added accountability and encouragement.
- **Be kind to yourself:** Finally, remember to be kind and compassionate to yourself throughout this process. It's normal to encounter challenges and setbacks along the way, but try not to judge yourself harshly. Instead, approach your practice with a sense of curiosity, patience, and self-compassion.

Remember that each moment of meditation and self-care is an opportunity for growth and self-discovery.

As you begin to integrate these self-care practices into your daily life, you may notice subtle yet significant changes in how you perceive yourself and your surroundings. Taking time for self-care not only nourishes your body and mind but also paves the way for a deeper connection with your inner self. This growing sense of balance and well-being creates the perfect foundation for cultivating greater self-awareness and once you harness this newfound clarity, you can better understand your thoughts, emotions, and behaviors, ultimately guiding you toward a more mindful and intentional life.

CHAPTER 2

KNOW THYSELF

I love the [wo]man that can smile in trouble, that can gather strength from distress, and grow brave by reflection.
—*Thomas Paine*, The American Crisis

Julia Child's career path is a prime example of how discovering your passion can redefine your professional life. Child did not begin her career in the culinary arts. In fact, she worked in media and advertising before joining the OSS, where she served as a research assistant during World War II. It wasn't until she was in her thirties, after moving to France with her husband, that she discovered her love for cooking. Child enrolled in the prestigious Le Cordon Bleu cooking school in Paris, which was the beginning of her illustrious career as a chef, author, and television personality. Her nonlinear path shows that it's never too late to discover your true passion and turn it into a successful career.

More than twenty years into my professional career, I was participating in a face-to-face meeting for the team I was supporting. It was the first time this newly formed global team had physically come together as a collective with the primary goals of getting to know each other better and gelling as one team. To facilitate this, the agenda for day one included an icebreaker activity that asked everyone to generate three to five "I am" statements about themselves to share with the others randomly assigned to their tables. A seemingly simple task—or so I thought.

To say my mind went blank would be misleading. I actually didn't even have any "I am" statements in my mind. I took a small amount of comfort in observing that I wasn't the only one struggling with this assignment. Blank stares surrounded me. Anxious whispers of "What are we supposed to be doing?" followed. Like school students whose teacher had just announced a pop quiz, some even resorting to asking others at our table "What are you going to say?"

I can only speak for myself; my struggle was real. Why was I having such a difficult time articulating who I was and what I stood for? Why was this exercise such a source of anxiety?

I wish I could tell you I had a moment of clarity in that meeting and the "I am" statements flowed effortlessly from my soul to my lips and into my colleagues' ears like feathers floating on a breeze. No such luck. My turning point came over a year later, soon after I found myself impacted by organizational restructuring and without a job.

Up to this point, I had often put others' needs before my own and found myself with little to nothing left for me. My energy was spent ensuring everyone around me was happy and taken care of. Me, myself, and I were very rarely considered, let alone catered to, in the holistic equation of my life.

This is not unique to me, as research shows that women often prioritize others' needs over their own, a tendency shaped by both cultural expectations and personal habits. For instance, societal norms frequently place women in caregiving roles, both professionally and personally, leading them to self-sabotage by neglecting their own well-being while taking care of others. This behavior is reinforced by learned patterns from early childhood and is often seen as a virtue, although it can have negative consequences on women's health and personal development. Moreover, the concept of altruism, especially as it pertains to women, has been studied extensively. Research indicates that women are more likely than men to engage in prosocial behaviors, including putting others' needs before their own, due to both biological and social influences. This tendency, while often admired, can lead to a depletion of personal resources and a sense of self-neglect.[2]

My being for the preceding fifteen years was defined by the roles I played for everyone except me. Doting wife and mom topped the list, while family breadwinner, good daughter, compassionate friend, and big sister closely followed. I could easily point out who I was for others, but when it came down to pointing out who I was for myself, I didn't have a clue.

How You Spend Your Time and Energy

As I reflect on my journey of self-discovery and the importance of understanding oneself, it's clear that the way we allocate our time and energy plays a pivotal role in shaping our identities. The balance between caring for others and caring for ourselves is delicate, and often it is skewed in favor of external responsibilities, leaving our own needs unmet. This imbalance, rooted in societal norms and reinforced by personal experiences, can lead to a disconnection from our true selves. It's in recognizing this pattern and reclaiming our own space in the equation of life that we begin to realign with our deeper sense of purpose and fulfillment. Meaning is a deeply personal and subjective concept, one that is as diverse and multifaceted as each of us who seek it. For me, meaning is found in the pursuit of creative expression,

---

[2] Janine Garner, "Why Do Women Always Put the Needs of Others Before Their Own?" Women's Agenda, August 4, 2013, https://womensagenda.com.au/life/jugglehood/why-do-women-always-put-the-needs-of-others-before-their-own/; "Prioritizing Care for Others, Women Often Neglect their Own Health," Go Red for Women, American Heart Association, November 10, 2020, https://www.goredforwomen.org/en/beyond-the-table/stories/women-often-neglect-their-own-health; Juris G. Draguns, "Altruism in its Personal, Social, and Cultural Contexts: An Introduction," in *Altruism in Cross-Cultural Perspective*, ed. D. Vakoch (New York: Springer, 2013), 1–16, https://doi.org/10.1007/978-1-4614-6952-0_1.

in the act of bringing something new and beautiful into the world. Whether it's being the first person in a new role or baking something delicious, I get a sense of euphoria and exhilaration when my work allows me to express myself authentically. This euphoria leads to inspiration that propels me forward in new experiences.

Others find meaning in service to others, in the profound sense of fulfillment that comes from making a positive impact on the lives of those around them. My mom was a social worker for years, dedicating herself to helping juvenile delinquents and impoverished older people. In her retirement, she became a hospice volunteer, inspired by the organization's mission and the compassion they showed to our family in the final days of my grandmother's life. She often speaks of the deep sense of purpose and satisfaction she receives from this work, as it enables her to contribute to the greater good, foster connections, and create positive change in her community.

Still others derive meaning from the pursuit of mastery, the relentless pursuit of excellence, and the continuous refinement of their skills and abilities. When Slash, the lead guitarist for Guns N' Roses, decided to dedicate himself to playing guitar, he practiced for up to twelve hours a day. Time seemed to stand still, and every action flowed effortlessly from one to the next as he immersed himself completely in the task at hand.

Why You Do It

Imagine your life as a grand tapestry, woven with threads of various hues and textures, each representing a different aspect of your existence. Among these threads are the activities you engage in, the pursuits you follow, and the passions that ignite your soul. Yet, many people never really pause to ponder why certain activities resonate with them more deeply than others. Have you explored the underlying reasons behind your affinity for specific jobs or hobbies? I never had until external circumstances forced it upon me.

Simon Sinek, a renowned thinker and author, delves deep into this fundamental query in his groundbreaking book *Start with Why*. He argues that great leaders and organizations don't just focus on what they do or how they do it; instead, they start with why. They understand that the essence of their existence lies not in the product they sell or the service they provide, but in the driving force behind it all—their purpose, their cause, their beliefs.[3] Similarly, each of us can benefit immensely from embracing this principle in our personal lives. By asking ourselves why we are drawn to certain activities, hobbies, or endeavors, we unearth a treasure trove of insight into our deepest motivations and aspirations.

To understand the significance behind your chosen activities means to decipher the map of your inner landscape. It offers you a glimpse into the intricate workings of your psyche, revealing the patterns and connections that shape your sense of purpose and fulfillment. Consider, for instance, that the avid reader who devours book after book may initially seem driven by a passion for storytelling or a thirst for knowledge. Yet, upon introspection, they may discover that their why extends far beyond mere entertainment or intellectual stimulation. Perhaps they are drawn to literature because it provides solace in times of turmoil, sparks empathy for human experience, or ignites a lifelong quest for truth and understanding.

Think about the activities that bring you joy, the tasks that make time seem to evaporate, and the endeavors that leave you feeling invigorated and alive. These are not coincidences. They are windows into your innermost desires and aspirations that hold the key to unlocking the mysteries of your personal meaning and identity. By delving into the why behind your chosen activities, you embark on a journey of self-discovery and self-realization. You uncover the unique blend of talents, values, and passions that define who you are and what truly matters to you. Armed with this reflective insight, you can navigate

---

[3] Simon Sinek, *Start with Why: How Great Leaders Inspire Everyone to Take Action*, (New York: Penguin, 2009).

the vast expanse of life with clarity and purpose, making choices that align with your authentic self and lead to a deeper sense of fulfillment.

Don't Have to Focus on One

One of the questions I get asked most often is, "How did you figure out what you wanted to do?" Honestly, I wish I could say that I had it all figured out from the start. But the truth is, my path has been anything but straightforward. It took countless hours of self-reflection, a series of trial-and-error experiences, the guidance of some incredibly insightful coaches, and a lot of patience before I finally began to see a clearer picture of my journey.

But there's one moment that stands out as a turning point—an experience that truly changed the way I understood myself and my career. It all started one afternoon when I was scrolling through LinkedIn, feeling the usual mix of inspiration and overwhelm that often accompanies seeing other people's success stories. That's when I stumbled upon a TED Talk by Emilie Wapnick titled "Why Some of Us Don't Have One True Calling." The title itself felt like it was speaking directly to me. Intrigued, I clicked play, and as I listened to Emilie describe the concept of the *multipotentialite*, it was like a lightbulb went off in my mind. For the first time, someone was putting into words the exact feelings I had been wrestling with for years—this idea that it's okay, even powerful, to have multiple passions and pursue different paths.

I was hooked. I listened to her words with a mix of excitement and relief. Here was someone who got me, who understood that my seemingly scattered interests and nonlinear career path weren't weaknesses, but rather strengths. Emilie's talk didn't just resonate; it validated my entire approach to life and work. It was like meeting a kindred spirit who was able to articulate what I had always felt but couldn't quite explain.

As soon as the talk ended, I knew I needed more. I immediately ordered her book, *How to Be Everything*, and when it arrived, I devoured it in just forty-eight hours. It was a revelation. Emilie's framework for "finding your whys" spoke directly to the heart of what I had been searching for. Her insights helped me understand that my diverse interests weren't a burden but a gift, and I could weave them together into a fulfilling, cohesive life. For the first time in forever, someone had managed to capture the essence of what I had been feeling for so long, and I felt empowered to embrace my identity as a multipotentialite.[4]

Embracing my identity as a multipotentialite was just the beginning. With Emilie's framework as my guide, I began to see the intricate connections between my various interests and how they could coexist harmoniously rather than compete for my attention. This newfound clarity didn't just change the way I viewed my past; it also transformed how I approached my future. I realized that the key to unlocking my true potential lay in understanding the deeper motivations that drove me to pursue different paths. With this insight, I felt a strong urge to share what I had learned with others who might be struggling with similar challenges. This desire to help others navigate their own journeys led me to develop a framework of my own, one that blends several different methodologies into a cohesive approach for finding your personal "whys," your identity.

A Framework for Finding Your Identity

Knowing yourself involves looking at how you spend your time and energy. And the good news is you don't have to focus on only one activity.

But it goes beyond just how and what you do and extends into why you do it. This gets at your core. To find your identity, follow these steps.

---

[4] Emilie Wapnick, *How to Be Everything: A Guide for Those Who (Still) Don't Know What They Want to Be When They Grow Up* (New York: HarperOne, 2017).

Identify Your What(s)

Reflect on your skills, strengths, values, and passions. Take time to quiet your mind through meditation, limit distractions, and really ponder all the things that make you uniquely you by asking yourself the following questions:

- What are the key skills and strengths that set me apart from others?
- What are the nonnegotiable values that drive every decision I make?
- What truly fuels my soul and gets me out of bed each morning?

Identify Your Why(s)

Now you need to go behind what and determine the why. I identified key experiences I loved in my personal and professional lives and *why* I loved them.

Think back to a time when you felt you were in it to win it, totally in your zone, and unstoppable. What were you doing? Close your eyes and visualize as many details as possible about the surroundings and feelings associated with that experience. This moment can be either a personal moment or a professional one. When I did this exercise, I saw myself at a large circular table solutioning a major issue with an interdisciplinary team I was leading.

Once you identify the experience (planning a large event, reading a book about engineering, traveling, baking, writing code for new software . . .), zoom out. What was it about the activity that made you feel alive? Why were you drawn to it? In my case, what I loved about my time leading that team was not solutioning major issues. It was the act of creative expression and personal growth. That large circular table was a place where I could think creatively to push status quo boundaries, engage in holistic problem-solving, and broaden my knowledge base by interacting with experts. To this day, I continue to seek out experiences that involve creative expression and personal growth. It doesn't matter if the work takes the form of traveling the world, baking, or accepting a newly created professional role. Each medium is just a different vehicle for creative expression and personal growth.

Repeat the above process for three to five other moments that you loved. It's totally fine if your experiences are very different from each other. You were likely drawn to them for different reasons. On a new page or a separate area of your existing page, make a list of the whys you uncovered.

Identify Common Themes

Now identify the common themes among all your experiences. If you used ChatGPT to help you identify your whys, find your common themes by entering the following prompt: "*List the 5 common themes of the above outputs.*"

By evaluating my outputs as a collective, my common themes across my experiences were creative expression, personal growth and learning, building connections and communities, and making a positive impact. These whys translate to the attributes of future professional roles and life experiences that will bring me the most joy and satisfaction.

> I am someone who embraces technology in any way I can to increase my efficiency and maximize my time. Once I identified my specific activities, I used ChatGPT to help give form to what I loved about each. For example, I entered the prompt "List 5 unique reasons why people love leading interdisciplinary teams." This provided me with a starting point to begin evaluating different reasons and see if any resonated with me. If they did, I captured them on my list. If they didn't, I prompted ChatGPT to provide me with more reasons ("Give me 5 more unique reasons why people love leading interdisciplinary teams") until I felt satisfied with my list. I repeated this process for each of my experiences.

Define Your UVP

Oprah Winfrey's career is a masterclass in crafting a UVP. Oprah began her career as a television news anchor and reporter, but she struggled with the limitations of traditional news formats, which didn't align with her strengths in storytelling and connecting with people on a deeper emotional level. In 1984 she took a significant risk by transitioning to hosting a morning talk show in Chicago, *A.M. Chicago*, which was later renamed *The Oprah Winfrey Show*.

Oprah's UVP was her ability to create a space where people felt safe to share their personal stories. Her authentic and empathetic interviewing style resonated with audiences, differentiating her from other talk show hosts. She turned this into a media empire, launching her own production company, Harpo Productions, and later her own television network, OWN.

Defining your UVP can be challenging because it requires a deep understanding of what sets you apart from others in a competitive landscape. Many people struggle with this because it involves introspection and self-awareness, which can be difficult to achieve without guidance. Often, individuals have a hard time identifying their unique strengths and how these can provide specific value to others. The pressure to distill complex skills and experiences into a concise and compelling statement can make the process even more daunting.

To make defining your UVP easier, reflect on your past successes and what others frequently seek you out for. Gathering feedback from colleagues, mentors, or clients can offer valuable insights into your strengths. Another helpful approach (and the reason defining your UVP is in the same section as finding your whys) is to consider your passions and what motivates you: these often align with your unique strengths and can help you articulate your UVP more authentically.

Finally, try to focus on the specific problems you solve or the benefits you offer, rather than just listing skills. By narrowing your focus and seeking external perspectives, you can craft a UVP that truly reflects your unique value. For example, my UVP is that my nonlinear and multidisciplinary career path has made me an expert in relating to different types of people and helping them relate to each other by translating between them. I effectively connect the dots across people, processes, and projects because I have so many different perspectives to draw from. Use the following questions as a starting point for your UVP statement:

- What sets you apart from others in terms of your perspective, problem-solving approach, and adaptability?
- If you have taken strength-finder assessments, like CliftonStrengths or DiSC, what have they said are your strengths?

Putting It All Together: Craft Your Personal Mission Statement

In his TED Talk "5 Steps to Building a Personal Brand You Feel Good About," Marcos Salazar outlines five key steps to building a personal brand that feels good.

- Figure out your goals
- Be clear on what you want to be known for
- Know your audience
- Create a mission statement
- Build your personal brand online[5]

Figuring out your goals is as personal as your UVP. Consider your short-term and long-term aspirations. These could relate to your career, personal development, relationships, or contributions to

---

[5] Marcos Salazar, "5 Steps to Building a Personal Brand You Feel Good About," TED Talk, April 5, 2023, https://www.youtube.com/watch?v=ozMCb0wOnMU.

society. My goals are primarily career focused. For example, I desire to be a chief operating officer of a life sciences company by 2034.

Being clear on what you want to be known for will determine how you show up to the world, both in person and online. Reflect on how you want to impact others and the world around you. Do you want to inspire, lead, support, or create change? I want to be known for my multidisciplinary expertise and for creating positive change in the lives of others.

Once you know that, you can better determine your audience, who you want to share your personal brand with. Your personal brand is not about you. Yes, you read that right. Your personal brand is not about you. It's about the people you want to educate with the skills, knowledge, and value you can provide. Who you decide to focus on should be based on two things: your goals and those who can most benefit from them. Think about who can most gain from your insights and how exactly you can see yourself helping them. My audience is prospective employers and early to midcareer professionals with nonlinear career paths.

Here's where everything we have worked on to this point starts to come together. Your personal mission statement should clearly articulate the following:

- Who you are
- What you do
- Who you do it for
- The transformation you create

<u>Tips for Writing Your Mission Statement</u>

Be authentic: Ensure your statement truly reflects who you are and what you believe in.
Keep it concise: Aim for a clear and brief statement that is easy to remember.

Make it inspiring: Your mission statement should motivate you and others.

Review and revise: Revisit your mission statement periodically and make adjustments as needed to reflect your evolving goals and values.

Personal Mission Statement Template

I strive to [action/impact] by [how you intend to achieve this], guided by my values of [core values]. My goal is to [personal/professional goals], creating a positive impact on [specific groups or broader community]. I am committed to [how you will stay true to your mission].

Personal Mission Statement Example

My name is Kristin Jemison and I'm a business operations executive. I strive to enhance patients' lives around the world by optimizing the way matrixed teams work to bring added-value medicines to market. I empower others to lead so, collectively, we can grow into better versions of ourselves. I believe that when we work together as a collective community we thrive and the world is a better place.

Your mission statement may look very different from mine, depending on who you are in your career. Whatever it is, write it down and put it someplace prominent. You can use it to make decisions about how you'll speak about yourself when you first meet someone, interview, or network.

As you journey deeper into understanding yourself—through introspection, discovering your whys, and crafting a clear UVP and personal mission statement—you lay a solid foundation for aligning your life and work with your true purpose. But self-awareness and clarity of purpose are only the beginning. To truly leverage these insights in your career, it's crucial to not only know who you are but also to recognize and articulate the tangible impact you've made in your professional life. With a strong sense of self established, it's time to shift focus and explore the achievements that define your career, showcasing how your unique strengths and values have translated into real-world success.

CHAPTER 3

YOU ARE A STAR

I have learned that success is to be measured not so much by the position one has reached in life as by the obstacles which he has overcome while trying to succeed.
— Booker T. Washington, Up From Slavery

Recognizing your career accomplishments is not just about building a resume; it's about understanding your professional journey and the impact you've made. This self-awareness can significantly boost your confidence and help you articulate your value to current or prospective employers. It involves reflecting on significant contributions such as key projects and roles where your input made a difference, understanding how your actions benefited others, and creating a cohesive story that highlights your skills and achievements.

In today's competitive job market, the ability to identify and document your career accomplishments effectively is essential. Whether you're aiming for a promotion, seeking new opportunities, or preparing for a performance review, having a well-documented record of your achievements can set you apart. So take the time to go through this comprehensive framework for recognizing and recording your professional milestones.

Taking a role-by-role career inventory to highlight professional accomplishments can be both intimidating and daunting. It was for me. For starters, early in my career I just didn't know how to recognize and distinguish between my just-doing-my-job accomplishments and my most impactful and influential ones. What criteria should I use to distinguish my good work from my great work? I didn't have a clue.

This ambiguity only fueled my procrastination; I waited until I had an interview scheduled to think about what I did in my preceding roles so I could speak to it. I repeatedly put myself in the pressured position of having to dig deep into the archives of my mind to remember years of my career in short time. This was stressful because I was forced to both identify my good versus great accomplishments and recall the specifics associated with an accomplishment in a short period. And did I even have great accomplishments? Who says they're great? Fear of judgment and impostor syndrome, the pervasive feeling of self-doubt and the belief that one's success is undeserved, affected me deeply. I often downplayed my achievements, giving credit to others over myself. Wasn't it always about the team? I would worry that I would come across as boastful or that my accomplishments would be scrutinized and found lacking. This fear of negative judgment also discouraged me from highlighting my achievements. And how many did I need? Could I have a list that applied to any and every job I would interview for, or did I need to categorize my accomplishments so I could strategically select the most applicable ones to highlight for a given role?

All these unknowns and more led me to keep a career journal.

Keep a Career Journal

A career journal is a personal record where you regularly note down your professional activities, accomplishments, and reflections. It is more than just a personal record—it's a powerful tool that can significantly enhance your professional life. By regularly documenting your professional activities, achievements, and reflections, you create a resource that can drive your career forward in several ways.

Benefits of Keeping a Career Journal

This practice offers several benefits:

- **Enhanced self-awareness:** Regularly recording your experiences helps you gain deeper insights into your strengths, areas for improvement, and career trajectory. It fosters a habit of self-reflection, making you more aware of your professional growth and development.
- **Accurate documentation:** A career journal ensures that you have a detailed and accurate record of your accomplishments. Instead of relying on memory when updating your resume or preparing for an interview, you can refer to your journal for specific details and examples.
- **Improved performance reviews:** Documenting your achievements throughout the year makes it easier to prepare for performance reviews. You can provide concrete examples of your contributions, making a stronger case for promotions, raises, or bonuses.
- **Goal setting and tracking:** A career journal allows you to set professional goals and track your progress. By regularly reviewing your entries, you can see how far you've come and identify areas where you need to focus more effort.
- **Stress reduction:** Keeping a journal can reduce stress by providing a structured way to process your experiences and emotions. It offers a private space to reflect on challenges and celebrate successes, contributing to your overall well-being.
- **Gain deeper insights and drive professional growth:** Recording your experiences in a career journal offers much more than a simple log of activities. It helps you develop a keen awareness of your strengths, areas for improvement,

and overall career trajectory. Through regular self-reflection, you cultivate a deeper understanding of your professional development, making you more intentional about your growth. For example, I've found that by reflecting on my tasks and projects weekly, I've identified patterns in my work that either highlight my strengths or expose areas needing improvement. This awareness has empowered me to take proactive steps in my career, such as seeking out specific training or mentorship opportunities to bolster areas where I felt less confident.

- **Build a robust repository of achievements:** One of the most practical benefits of maintaining a career journal is having a detailed, accurate record of your accomplishments. Instead of scrambling to remember your successes when updating your resume or preparing for an interview, you have a ready-made, comprehensive list. This not only saves time but also significantly reduces the stress associated with these tasks. Imagine you're preparing for an annual performance review. With a career journal, you can easily pull up specific examples of projects you led, challenges you overcame, and the impact you made. This makes it easier to advocate for promotions or raises because you can clearly demonstrate your value. In fact, studies show that women who actively document their accomplishments and advocate for themselves are more likely to receive promotions. Women who build a case for their achievements, for example, are 20 percent more likely to be promoted than those who wait for someone else to recognize their efforts.
- **Enhance emotional well-being and reduce stress:** Beyond its professional benefits, a career journal can be a valuable tool for managing stress and enhancing emotional well-being. The act of writing about your experiences, especially challenging ones, provides a structured way to process your emotions. By reflecting on these experiences, you can gain

perspective, celebrate your successes, and constructively learn from setbacks. For instance, I've used my journal to process difficult interactions with colleagues or to work through the stress of tight project deadlines. Writing about these situations helps me clear my mind and approach future challenges with a calmer, more strategic mindset.

Best Practices for Establishing a Career Journal

To maximize the benefits of a career journal, consistency and organization are key.

- **Consistency:** Make journaling a regular habit. Whether weekly or monthly, set aside dedicated time to update your journal. Consistent entries ensure that no achievements or lessons learned slip through the cracks.
- **Detail-oriented entries:** Don't just note down what you did—include specifics like dates, project names, key tasks, outcomes, and your role. The more detailed your entries, the more useful they will be later.
- **Reflection:** Move beyond listing tasks. Reflect on what you learned, how you overcame challenges, and how each experience contributed to your professional growth. This reflection is where the true value of a career journal lies.
- **Organization:** Organize your journal with sections or categories, such as projects, skills, feedback, and goals. This makes it easier to review and use your entries when needed.

Create Your Career Accomplishments, the STAR Method

The STAR method is a structured approach to documenting accomplishments that translate well to interviews and performance reviews. STAR stands for situation, task, action, and result. Let's break down each component and explore the psychology behind why this method is effective.

- **Situation:** Describe the context or background of your accomplishment. This sets the stage and provides the interviewer or evaluator with a clear understanding of the circumstances. *Psychological aspect:* Providing context helps the listener visualize the scenario, making your story more relatable and engaging. It establishes the relevance of your accomplishment.
- **Task:** Explain the specific task or challenge you were faced with. This should include your responsibilities and the goals you needed to achieve. *Psychological aspect:* Highlighting the task clarifies your role and the expectations placed on you. It demonstrates your ability to identify and understand key challenges.
- **Action:** Detail the actions you took to address the task or challenge. Focus on what you did, how you did it, and the skills you used. *Psychological aspect:* Discussing your actions showcases your problem-solving abilities and proactive behavior. It emphasizes your competencies and decision-making skills.
- **Result:** Share the outcomes of your actions. Quantify the results if possible, using metrics such as percentages, numbers, or other concrete data. *Psychological aspect:* Presenting results provides tangible proof of your impact. Quantifiable outcomes make your accomplishments more credible and impressive, reinforcing your value to the organization.

Why the STAR Method Is Effective

The STAR method is widely recognized and used because it offers several advantages:

- **Clarity and structure:** The structured format ensures that your responses are clear and concise, preventing you from rambling or going off-topic. It helps you present your achievements logically and compellingly.
- **Demonstrates competency:** By breaking down your accomplishments into situation, task, action, and result, you effectively demonstrate your competencies. This method highlights not only what you achieved but also how you achieved it, showcasing your skills and abilities.
- **Enhances credibility:** Including specific details and quantifiable results enhances the credibility of your accomplishments. It provides concrete evidence of your contributions, making your claims more convincing.
- **Engages the listener:** The narrative structure of the STAR method makes your stories more engaging and memorable. It helps the listener follow your thought process and understand the significance of your achievements.

Practical Tips for Using the STAR Method

To effectively use the STAR method, consider the following tips:

- **Be specific:** Avoid vague statements. Provide clear and specific details for each component of the method.
- **Quantify results:** Include numbers, percentages, or other quantifiable data to illustrate your results. Whenever possible, follow the money.
- **Practice:** Prepare and practice your STAR stories in advance. This will help you feel more confident and articulate during interviews or performance reviews.
- **Tailor to the audience:** Adapt your STAR stories to the specific job or context. Highlight the skills and achievements most relevant to the position or situation.

Bad, Good, Great

Use the examples below to get an idea of what distinguishes bad from great STAR-method accomplishments.

Bad Example

- **Situation:** At my last job, I was part of a project team.
- **Task:** I was responsible for making sure things went smoothly.
- **Action:** I worked hard with the team and did my best to help out.
- **Result:** We finished the project.

This example is vague and lacks specifics. The situation doesn't provide enough context, the task is too broad, the actions taken are not clearly described, and the result is ambiguous. Without concrete details, it's impossible to gauge the significance of the accomplishment or the individual's contribution.

Good Example

- **Situation:** At my last job, our sales team was facing a significant decline in customer retention, which was affecting our revenue.
- **Task:** I was assigned to develop and implement a strategy to improve customer retention rates.
- **Action:** I conducted a thorough analysis of customer feedback to identify the main issues. Based on this analysis, I developed a new customer engagement program that included regular follow-ups, personalized service, and a loyalty rewards system. I also trained the sales team on these new initiatives.
- **Result:** As a result, our customer retention rate increased by 25 percent over six months, and we saw a 15 percent increase in revenue.

This example is much clearer and provides specific details about the situation, task, actions, and results. The situation sets the context, the task outlines the individual's responsibility, the actions describe what was done to address the problem, and the results quantify the success. This makes the accomplishment more credible and highlights the individual's impact.

Great Example

- **Situation:** At my previous job as a senior sales manager at XYZ Corporation, the company faced a significant challenge with customer retention, which had dropped to 60 percent, leading to a 10 percent decrease in annual revenue.
- **Task:** I was tasked with developing and implementing a comprehensive strategy to improve customer retention rates and restore revenue growth.
- **Action:** I initiated a detailed analysis of customer feedback and sales data to identify pain points. Based on these insights, I designed a multifaceted customer engagement program that included the following:

    - *Personalized follow-ups*: I implemented a customer relationship management system to track customer interactions and schedule personalized follow-ups based on individual customer needs.
    - *Loyalty rewards program*: I launched a tiered loyalty program offering exclusive discounts, early access to new products, and personalized offers.
    - *Training and development*: I conducted workshops and training sessions for the sales team to enhance their customer service skills and familiarize them with the new engagement program.

- *Feedback loop*: I established a continuous feedback loop with customers to regularly gather insights and adjust strategies as needed.
- **Result:** As a result of these initiatives, customer retention rates improved from 60 percent to 85 percent within six months, surpassing our initial target. This increase in retention contributed to a 20 percent rise in annual revenue. Additionally, customer satisfaction scores improved by 30 percent, and we received several testimonials praising the enhanced customer experience.

This great example stands out due to its comprehensive and detailed approach. The situation is described with specific metrics, providing a clear understanding of the challenge. The task is clearly defined, outlining the responsibility of the individual. The actions are detailed and broken down into specific initiatives, showcasing a well-rounded strategy and highlighting various skills such as data analysis, program design, and team training. The results are quantifiable and exceed expectations, demonstrating a significant impact. This level of detail and clarity makes the accomplishment highly credible and impressive.

Great Example: Project Management

- **Situation:** At my previous job, our team was struggling with delayed project deadlines, which affected client satisfaction and revenue.
- **Task:** I was assigned to lead a project aimed at improving our project management processes and reducing delays.
- **Action:** I implemented new project management software, trained the team on its use, and restructured our workflow to improve efficiency. I also introduced weekly progress meetings to ensure timely updates and address issues promptly.

- **Result:** As a result, we reduced project delays by 40 percent within six months, improved client satisfaction scores by 30 percent, and increased overall revenue by 15 percent.

Great Example: Customer Service Improvement

- **Situation:** Our customer service department received numerous complaints about response times and issue resolution.
- **Task:** I was tasked with improving the efficiency and effectiveness of our customer service operations.
- **Action:** I conducted a thorough analysis of our existing processes, identified bottlenecks, and implemented a new ticketing system. I also organized training sessions to enhance the team's problem-solving skills and introduced a customer feedback loop to continuously monitor and improve our service.
- **Result:** Within three months, our average response time decreased by 50 percent, issue resolution rates improved by 35 percent, and customer satisfaction scores increased by 20 percent.

Key Takeaways

- **Specificity and detail:** Providing detailed descriptions and specific metrics enhances the credibility and impact of the accomplishment.
- **Clear context:** Setting the stage with a well-defined situation helps the listener understand the significance of the challenge.
- **Concrete actions:** Clearly outlining the steps taken to address the task demonstrates problem-solving skills and initiative.
- **Quantifiable results:** Using numbers to illustrate the outcome makes the accomplishment tangible and easy to understand.

- **Comprehensive approach:** An exceptional example often includes multiple actions and initiatives, showcasing a range of skills and a strategic approach.

By following these guidelines, you can effectively use the STAR method to articulate your career accomplishments, making them compelling and memorable to prospective employers or evaluators.

Amplify Your Career Journal with the STAR Method

Integrating the STAR method into your career journaling can amplify its effectiveness.

- **Regular entries using the STAR format:** Document your accomplishments using the STAR format. This keeps your records structured and helps you practice articulating your achievements in a compelling manner—perfect for performance reviews or interviews.
- **Reflection and analysis:** Periodically review your STAR entries to reflect on your growth. Analyze the situations, tasks, actions, and results to gain deeper insights into your professional development.
- **Preparation for reviews and interviews:** Your journal becomes an invaluable resource when preparing for performance reviews, job interviews, or networking events. With well-documented STAR stories, you'll always be ready to showcase your accomplishments confidently and effectively.

Keeping a career journal is a strategic practice that offers a multitude of benefits—from deepening self-awareness and reducing stress to enhancing performance reviews and increasing the likelihood of promotions. By documenting your professional journey and integrating methods like STAR, you build a strong narrative of your career that can open doors to new opportunities and successes. Remember, your career is a story in progress; write it well, and it will lead you to the future you envision.

Now that you've identified and documented your career accomplishments, you've laid a solid foundation for the next critical step in your professional development: crafting your career narrative. In today's dynamic job market, where nonlinear career paths are increasingly common, effectively weaving together your diverse experiences into a coherent and compelling story is more important than ever. A well-crafted career narrative not only showcases your unique journey but also connects the dots between seemingly disparate roles and industries, highlighting the skills and insights you've gained along the way. This narrative is your opportunity to present a clear and engaging picture of your professional evolution, making it easier for potential employers, colleagues, and networks to understand and appreciate the value you bring to the table.

CHAPTER 4

CREATE YOUR CAREER NARRATIVE

The best way to predict the future is to invent it.
— *Alan Kay*

Narrative writing is the art of storytelling, where experiences and events are presented in a structured, coherent manner to convey meaning, evoke emotions, and engage the audience. At its core, narrative writing involves a clear beginning, middle, and end, with a central theme or message that ties the story together. In literature, this technique allows authors to create compelling tales that resonate with readers, providing both entertainment and insight.

The principles of narrative writing are equally applicable to crafting a cohesive career narrative. Just as a good story weaves various events and character developments together into a meaningful plot, a well-crafted career narrative connects disparate job experiences and roles into a unified professional journey. This narrative can effectively communicate to potential employers not only your career path but your skills, values, and aspirations as well.

"Tell me about yourself" is usually one of the first questions asked to break the ice in professional interviews. How many times have you regurgitated an abbreviated version of your resume when answering? I can't count how many times I have. I assumed that if a person in a professional setting asked this, they wanted to know about me professionally. And, in part, they do. But believe me when I tell you they would also love for you to seize this opportunity to differentiate yourself from the competition and leave them feeling confident they got it right when they asked you to interview for this role. A well-defined career narrative helps potential employers understand your career trajectory, making it easier for them to see how your experiences and skills align with the job you are applying for. In a competitive job market, highlighting the unique value you bring to the table in an articulate, memorable way sets you apart and gives you a distinct advantage over others who recount to the interviewer what is already on the resume.

Crafting a compelling career narrative involves weaving together the various threads of your professional journey into a cohesive and engaging story. This process can be broken down into three main elements: the introduction, the body, and the conclusion. Each element plays a crucial role in ensuring that your narrative is clear, logical, and impactful.

Introduction

The introduction of your career narrative is like the opening scene of a movie—it sets the stage and provides essential context for what follows. This section is critical, as it gives your audience an initial glimpse into who you are, where you started, and what has motivated you along the way. A well-crafted introduction establishes a strong foundation for your narrative, making the rest of your story more compelling and relatable. It should capture the essence of your early career motivations and the initial steps that defined your professional journey.

Background

Begin by exploring what initially drew you to your field. This isn't just about stating your interests; it's about painting a vivid picture of the passion or curiosity that sparked your career. Were you the kind of person who dismantled gadgets as a child to understand how they worked, leading to a lifelong passion for engineering? Or perhaps a specific event or mentor in your life ignited a desire to help others, steering you toward a career in healthcare or education.

For example, if you pursued a career in environmental science, you might describe a pivotal moment from your youth, such as witnessing the impact of pollution on your local community, which fueled your commitment to environmental stewardship. By connecting your personal experiences with your career motivations, you provide a strong foundation that explains your career choices and sets the stage for the rest of your narrative.

Concrete Steps

Next, delve into the concrete steps you took as you embarked on your career. This section should outline your educational background, any significant training or certifications, and your early professional experiences. Highlight the key decisions you made, the opportunities you seized, and the challenges you overcame. These elements should illustrate not just what you did but why those decisions were pivotal in shaping your career trajectory. If you started your career with an internship at a major tech company, discuss how that experience solidified your interest in software development and provided you with essential skills and insights that guided your subsequent career moves. Mention any mentors or significant projects during this time that influenced your path, and reflect on how these early experiences laid the groundwork for your future success. By clearly defining these initial steps, you help the reader understand the strategic thinking and purpose behind your career journey.

Body

The body of your career narrative is where you detail the various roles and experiences that have contributed to your professional growth. This section should be organized chronologically or thematically, with each role building on the previous one to demonstrate a clear path of development.

Responsibilities

It's not just about listing jobs; it's about telling the story of your evolution as a professional. For each major role in your career, provide an overview of your responsibilities. This isn't just about listing your duties—it's about contextualizing your contributions within the larger framework of the organization and industry. Describe the scope of your work, the size and nature of the teams you led, the complexity of the projects you handled, and the challenges you faced. This level of detail helps the reader understand the breadth and depth of your experience. For example, if you were a project manager, don't just say you managed projects. Instead, describe the types of projects (e.g., large-scale infrastructure, software development, or marketing campaigns), the budgets you handled, and the stakeholders you coordinated with. Explain how your role fits into the larger goals of the organization and how your responsibilities evolved over time. This approach not only clarifies your role but also highlights your ability to manage complexity and drive results.

Achievements

Your achievements are the heart of your career narrative's body. Here, you should highlight your significant accomplishments in each role, providing specific examples and, where possible, quantifiable metrics. These achievements are the proof points of your narrative, demonstrating the impact you've made throughout your career. When discussing achievements, focus on those that showcase your unique strengths and contributions. For example, instead of just saying you improved sales, specify how you did it—perhaps you led a targeted marketing campaign that resulted in a 20 percent increase in sales over six months, or you implemented a new customer relationship management system that reduced customer churn by 15 percent. These concrete details provide evidence of your effectiveness and ability to deliver results, making your narrative more compelling and believable.

Skills Developed

Discuss the skills you developed in each role, emphasizing how they have contributed to your professional growth and are relevant to your future goals. This includes both technical skills (like proficiency in specific software tools, data analysis, or project management) and soft skills (such as leadership, communication, or problem-solving). For instance, if a role required you to lead cross-functional teams, you might discuss how this experience honed your leadership and collaboration skills, preparing you for higher-level management positions. Or, if a position involved learning and applying new technologies, explain how you've continued to stay at the forefront of industry developments, making you an asset in any tech-driven environment. By framing your skills in the context of your career progression, you show how each role has prepared you for future challenges and opportunities.

Conclusion

The conclusion of your career narrative is where you tie everything together, summarizing your journey and positioning yourself for the next step in your career. This section is about reinforcing the coherence of your narrative and making a strong case for your candidacy or next career move.

Summary

Begin by providing a concise summary of your career journey, reiterating the central theme or themes that tie your experiences together. This could be a consistent focus on innovation, a commitment to customer service, or a track record of leadership. The goal here is to distill your narrative into a few key messages that resonate with your audience. You might summarize by highlighting how your career has been defined by a continuous pursuit of excellence in project management, leading to successful outcomes in diverse industries. This summary not only reinforces the coherence of your narrative but also makes it easier for others to understand and remember your career story.

Future Goals

Connect your past experiences to your future aspirations, explaining how your unique background makes you a strong candidate for your next role. This is where you articulate your vision for the future and how your past experiences have prepared you to achieve it. If your goal is to transition into a leadership role in a new industry, explain how your diverse experience across different sectors has equipped you with the adaptability and strategic thinking needed to lead in that environment. Or, if you're aiming for a specialized role, discuss how your past work has built the specific expertise required for success. By linking your career history to your future goals, you present a forward-looking narrative that positions you as a strong candidate for the opportunities ahead.

Call to Action

Conclude with a strong, positive statement that underscores your enthusiasm and readiness for the next challenge. This could be an expression of excitement about the opportunities ahead and a confident assertion of your ability to contribute to your target organization. You might end by saying, "I am excited to bring my experience in driving strategic initiatives and leading cross-functional teams to a new role where I can continue to deliver impactful results." This closing statement leaves the reader with a clear sense of your direction and motivation, making a lasting impression that reinforces the overall strength of your career narrative.

By crafting a compelling introduction, a detailed body, and a strong conclusion, you create a career narrative that not only highlights your past achievements but also positions you for future success. This structured approach ensures that your career story is not just a list of jobs and skills but a cohesive and engaging narrative that showcases your unique value.

Craft Your Career Narrative

Creating a cohesive career narrative requires introspection, organization, and strategic thinking. The following framework provides a step-by-step approach to help you craft your own nonlinear career narrative.

Step 1: Self-Assessment and Reflection

Start by conducting a thorough self-assessment to understand your career journey and what has driven you at each stage. Reflect on the following questions:

- What are your core skills and strengths?
- What motivates you professionally?
- What are your key achievements and milestones?
- What lessons have you learned from your various roles?
- How have your experiences shaped your career goals?

Document your answers and look for patterns or themes that emerge. This will help you identify the central theme of your career narrative.

Step 2: Identify Your Central Theme

A central theme ties your diverse experiences together and provides a coherent storyline. Choose a theme that resonates with your experiences and aligns with your career goals. Common themes include:

- **Adaptability:** Emphasize how your varied roles have made you adaptable and resilient.
- **Continuous learning:** Highlight your commitment to learning and personal growth throughout your career.
- **Problem-solving:** Focus on your ability to tackle diverse challenges and find innovative solutions.

Step 3: Structure Your Narrative

With your central theme in mind, outline the structure of your career narrative:

Introduction

- **Background and early career:** Explain what initially drew you to your field and the motivations behind your first job choice.
- **Concrete steps:** Briefly describe your educational background and early career decisions.

Body

Break down your career into key experiences or phases. For each role, highlight:

- **Role and responsibilities:** Describe your job title, key duties, and the context of the role.
- **Achievements:** Focus on specific accomplishments and how they contributed to your growth.
- **Skills developed:** Identify the skills you gained and how they are transferable to future roles.

Conclusion

- **Career summary:** Summarize your career journey, reiterating your central theme.
- **Future goals:** Connect your past experiences to your future aspirations, emphasizing how your diverse background makes you a strong fit for the target role.
- **Call to action:** End with a call to action.

Step 4: Craft the Narrative

Now, begin crafting your narrative, ensuring it is clear, concise, and engaging. Use this detailed example to guide you:

Introduction

My journey began with a passion for problem-solving and a curiosity about how things work. This passion led me to pursue a degree in mechanical engineering, where I honed my analytical skills and developed a solid foundation in technical knowledge. My first job as a junior engineer at XYZ Corporation was an exciting opportunity to apply my skills in a real-world setting.

Body

Phase 1: Engineering Beginnings

- **Role and responsibilities:** As a junior engineer, I was responsible for designing and testing mechanical components. I collaborated with senior engineers to develop innovative solutions for complex problems.
- **Achievements:** I successfully designed a new component that improved the efficiency of a key product by 15 percent. This achievement not only boosted my confidence but also earned me a promotion.
- **Skills developed:** I enhanced my technical skills, project management abilities, and teamwork. I learned the importance of precision, attention to detail, and the value of collaboration.

Phase 2: Transition to Project Management

- **Role and responsibilities:** I transitioned to a project management role at ABC Corp., overseeing cross-functional teams to deliver engineering projects on time and within budget.
- **Achievements:** I led a team that completed a major project three months ahead of schedule, resulting in significant cost savings for the company.
- **Skills developed:** I developed strong leadership, communication, and organizational skills and gained a deeper understanding of the business side of engineering and the importance of stakeholder management.

Phase 3: Exploring New Horizons in Tech

- **Role and responsibilities:** I moved to a tech startup as a product manager, where I was responsible for the entire product life cycle from conception to launch.
- **Achievements:** I successfully launched a new software product that became one of the company's top revenue generators within six months.
- **Skills developed:** I acquired new skills in software development, agile methodologies, and user experience design. I learned the value of adaptability, quick decision-making, and staying abreast of industry trends.

Conclusion

My career path, while nonlinear, has been driven by a continuous quest for learning and growth. The diverse roles I have undertaken have equipped me with a unique blend of technical expertise, project management skills, and product development experience. Moving forward, I am excited to leverage these skills in a senior product management role, where I can continue to drive innovation and deliver impactful solutions.

Step 5: Refine and Polish

After drafting your narrative, refine and polish it to ensure clarity and coherence:

- **Edit for conciseness:** Ensure your narrative is concise and to the point. Avoid unnecessary details that do not contribute to your central theme.
- **Use clear language:** Use clear and straightforward language. Avoid jargon unless it is relevant and understandable to your audience.

- **Seek feedback:** Share your narrative with trusted colleagues, mentors, or career coaches for feedback. They can provide valuable insights and help you improve your story.

Step 6: Prepare for Different Formats

For professionals with a nonlinear career path, tailoring your career narrative for different formats is essential. Unlike a traditional, linear career path where each role naturally leads to the next, a nonlinear career involves diverse experiences that may seem unrelated at first glance. Therefore, effectively communicating your unique journey requires careful adaptation to each platform or situation where your narrative will be shared. This tailored approach not only ensures clarity but also maximizes the impact of your story, making it relevant to the audience at hand. You can tailor your narrative depending on the format.

Resume

Your resume is often the first impression you make, so it needs to be concise, clear, and aligned with the job you're applying for. For someone with a nonlinear career path, this means strategically highlighting the most relevant aspects of your experience and downplaying any perceived gaps or unrelated roles.

Summary section: The summary section is your opportunity to introduce the overarching theme of your career narrative. Here, you can briefly touch on the diverse experiences you've had and how they've equipped you with a unique set of skills. For example, if you've transitioned from teaching to project management, your summary might emphasize your ability to communicate complex ideas clearly and manage diverse teams, skills that are valuable in both fields.

Experience section: In the experience section, you should focus on the roles that are most relevant to the job you're applying for. Use bullet points to highlight key achievements and skills that align with your narrative. For example, if you're applying for a marketing role but have a background in sales, highlight experiences where you successfully bridged the gap between the two, such as developing sales strategies that aligned with marketing campaigns. This not only shows your versatility but also how your diverse background adds value to the prospective role.

Cover Letter

A cover letter offers a more personal space to connect the dots of your nonlinear career path. It allows you to explain your transitions and the intentionality behind your career choices, making your narrative more relatable and compelling.

Introduction: Start with a compelling introduction that sets the stage for your narrative. If you've made significant career shifts, use this space to briefly explain what motivated those changes. For instance, if you transitioned from finance to nonprofit work, your introduction could discuss your growing desire to apply your financial expertise to causes you're passionate about, thus framing your diverse experiences as a strength rather than a series of unrelated jobs.

Body: In the body of the letter, expand on key experiences that relate directly to the position you're applying for. Use this section to tell a cohesive story about how your previous roles, although varied, have built a unique skill set that is perfectly suited for the new role. If you're moving into a leadership position, for example, you might discuss how your experience in different industries has given you a broad perspective on problem-solving and team management.

Conclusion: Conclude with a strong statement that connects your past experiences to your future goals. Emphasize how your nonlinear path has prepared you for the role and express enthusiasm for the opportunity to bring your unique perspective to the company. This not only reinforces the coherence of your narrative but also shows forward-thinking and confidence in your ability to succeed.

LinkedIn Profile

Your LinkedIn profile is a public-facing version of your career narrative that needs to be engaging, comprehensive, and keyword-optimized. Unlike a resume, LinkedIn allows for a more narrative-driven approach, making it an ideal platform to showcase the breadth of your experience.

Headline: Your headline should capture your UVP in a few words. For someone with a nonlinear career path, this might involve highlighting your interdisciplinary expertise or a particular skill that ties your experiences together. For example, "Bridging Education and Technology to Drive Innovative Solutions" could be a powerful headline for someone who has transitioned from teaching to tech.

About section: In the about section tell your career story in a more personal and engaging way. This is the place to elaborate on how your diverse experiences have shaped your professional identity. If your career path has taken you from journalism to corporate communications, you might discuss how your background in storytelling has enhanced your ability to craft compelling corporate narratives. Use this section to connect your past roles to your current professional focus, providing a clear and cohesive story that makes sense to your audience.

Experience section: Similar to your resume, the experience section should highlight your key roles and achievements. However, LinkedIn allows you to add more context, so take advantage of this by including a brief description of each role that explains how it fits into your overall career narrative. For instance, if you had a stint in customer service before moving into HR, explain how that experience honed your skills in employee relations and communication.

Interviews

In interviews, your career narrative needs to be adaptable and fluid, allowing you to respond effectively to a variety of questions. This is where you truly bring your narrative to life, demonstrating how your nonlinear path has prepared you for the role at hand.

Elevator pitch: Prepare a brief elevator pitch that encapsulates your career narrative in a compelling way. For someone with a nonlinear path, this pitch should focus on the unique value you bring because of your varied experiences. For example, you might say, "I've spent my career at the intersection of marketing and technology, leveraging my diverse background in sales, project management, and digital strategy to drive growth and innovation." This concise summary helps interviewers quickly understand the breadth of your experience and how it aligns with the position.

Behavioral questions: When responding to behavioral questions, use your narrative to structure your answers. Draw on experiences from different roles to illustrate how you've developed the skills the employer is looking for. For example, if asked about a time you led a team, you could share how your leadership style has evolved through managing teams in both nonprofit and corporate settings, demonstrating adaptability and a broad understanding of team dynamics. This approach not only answers the question but also reinforces the theme of your career narrative.

The Benefits of Tailoring Your Narrative

Tailoring your career narrative for different formats offers several key benefits, especially for those with nonlinear career paths:

- **Clarity:** A well-tailored narrative helps clarify how your diverse experiences connect and contribute to your current career goals, making it easier for employers to see the value you bring.
- **Relevance:** By highlighting the most relevant aspects of your experience for each format, you ensure that your narrative resonates with your audience, whether it's a hiring manager, a recruiter, or a professional network.

- **Consistency:** Tailoring doesn't mean changing your story; it means presenting it consistently across different platforms in a way that aligns with the specific expectations of each format. This consistency builds a strong, cohesive brand.
- **Engagement:** Tailoring your narrative for more narrative-driven formats like cover letters and LinkedIn profiles allows you to engage your audience on a deeper level, making your story more memorable and compelling.
- **Flexibility:** In interviews, being prepared with a tailored narrative allows you to pivot your responses based on the questions asked, ensuring that you always present your most relevant and impactful experiences.

Crafting a cohesive career narrative from a nonlinear path is both an art and a science. It requires introspection, strategic thinking, and the ability to weave together diverse experiences into a compelling story. By tailoring your narrative for different formats, you can create one that not only makes sense of your career journey but also positions you as a unique and valuable candidate in the eyes of future employers.

As you've learned to craft a compelling narrative that weaves together the diverse threads of your nonlinear career path, it's important to recognize that the power of your story is rooted not just in how you present your experiences but also in how you perceive and own them. Owning who you are and embracing the unique trajectory of your career is essential to building the confidence needed to make bold, intentional moves in your professional life.

CHAPTER 5

OWN IT

Own who you are and celebrate it.
—RuPaul

Steve Jobs, co-founder of Apple, is one of the most iconic figures who exemplified owning a nonlinear career path. After dropping out of Reed College, Jobs explored various interests, including calligraphy, which would later influence the typography of Apple products. His journey wasn't straightforward. In 1985, Jobs was famously ousted from Apple, the company he had co-founded. Instead of succumbing to defeat, he founded NeXT, a computer platform development company, and bought the Computer Division of Lucasfilm (later Pixar), which revolutionized the animation industry. Pixar's success eventually led to its acquisition by Disney.

In 1997, Jobs returned to Apple, which was on the brink of bankruptcy. His nonlinear experiences outside Apple, particularly with design and animation, played a crucial role in his ability to revitalize the company. The iMac, iPod, iPhone, and iPad were all products of Jobs's ability to blend technology with the arts, an approach he cultivated through his varied experiences. His career trajectory highlights the power of embracing a nonlinear path, where seemingly unrelated experiences can lead to groundbreaking innovation.

Psychological Resilience and Owning the Duality of Your Nonlinear Career

Embracing the breadth of your nonlinear career path is not solely about gathering diverse skills and experiences; it also involves psychologically owning the duality inherent in such a journey. This duality—where you simultaneously navigate different roles, industries, and skill sets—presents both challenges and opportunities. To thrive, you must build psychological resilience, which enables you to integrate and own the seemingly disparate elements of your career, transforming them into a cohesive and powerful narrative.

Owning this duality begins with a shift in how you perceive your career. Instead of viewing your varied experiences as disjointed or lacking focus, it's essential to see them as complementary parts of a larger, evolving story. This narrative integration allows you to derive meaning and value from each experience, reinforcing a sense of purpose and coherence in your professional journey. Research supports this approach, showing that individuals who find coherence in their career narratives are more likely to experience job satisfaction and psychological well-being.[6] By embracing both the creative and analytical aspects of your career, or the strategic and operational roles you've inhabited, you develop a multifaceted professional identity that is both versatile and resilient.

A critical aspect of this psychological ownership is the ability to embrace uncertainty. Nonlinear careers are often marked by unpredictability, which can trigger anxiety and self-doubt. However, resilience involves reframing this uncertainty as a source of strength. Embracing the duality of your career means acknowledging that the path forward is not always clear, but that this very ambiguity provides opportunities for growth and innovation. Studies in positive psychology suggest that individuals who view uncertainty as

---

[6] Dan P. McAdams and Kate C. McLean, "Narrative Identity," *Current Directions in Psychological Science* 22, no. 3 (2013): 233–238, https://doi.org/10.1177/0963721413475622.

an opportunity for exploration are more likely to develop adaptive coping strategies and achieve long-term success.[7] By accepting the dual nature of your career—where stability coexists with change and expertise is balanced with continual learning—you position yourself to thrive in dynamic environments.

Psychologically owning your nonlinear career also involves committing to continuous learning and self-improvement. The duality of your career path often requires you to develop new skills while simultaneously leveraging existing ones. To facilitate this ongoing process of growth, you need a growth mindset, as outlined by psychologist Carol Dweck. A growth mindset encourages you to see challenges as opportunities to expand your abilities, rather than as threats to your competence.[8] In the context of a nonlinear career, this mindset is essential for integrating the dual aspects of your professional identity, enabling you to adapt to new roles and environments with confidence.

Furthermore, social support plays a vital role in reinforcing psychological resilience and ownership of your career duality. Engaging with mentors, peers, and members of professional networks who understand and appreciate the value of a nonlinear career path can provide crucial validation and encouragement. These connections help you navigate the complexities of your dual career identity, offering insights and perspectives that reinforce the integration of your diverse experiences. Research has consistently shown that strong social networks can mitigate the stress associated with career transitions and uncertainties, further enhancing your resilience.[9]

---

[7] Barbara L. Fredrickson, "The Role of Positive Emotions in Positive Psychology: The Broaden-and-Build Theory of Positive Emotions," *American Psychologist* 56, no. 3 (2001): 218–226, https://doi.org/10.1037/0003-066X.56.3.218.

[8] Carol S. Dweck, *Mindset: The New Psychology of Success* (New York: Random House, 2006).

[9] Sheldon Cohen and Thomas A. Wills, "Stress, Social Support, and the Buffering Hypothesis," *Psychological Bulletin* 98, no. 2 (1985): 310–357, https://doi.org/10.1037/0033-2909.98.2.310.

Ultimately, psychologically owning your nonlinear career duality means accepting and embracing the multifaceted nature of your professional journey. This acceptance involves letting go of conventional career expectations and focusing instead on the unique opportunities that arise from your diverse experiences. By embracing this duality, you can cultivate a sense of agency and control over your career trajectory, even when it diverges from traditional paths. This psychological flexibility is essential for maintaining momentum and achieving long-term success in a world where adaptability and versatility are increasingly valued.

The Psychological Aspect of Owning Your Career Path

For years, I grappled with accepting the multifaceted nature of my career. Everywhere I looked, it seemed like everyone around me was a specialist, someone with deep expertise in a single area. Meanwhile, I often found myself finishing as the runner-up when competing against these specialists for roles. This constant comparison made me question my own path and wonder if my diverse interests and varied experiences were more of a hindrance than a strength. And after five months of unemployment, I was feeling increasingly anxious about what lay ahead. I had applied for over thirty jobs, secured just two interviews, and landed none. Despite applying for roles I was well qualified for, I received no responses. It was disheartening to spend hours on LinkedIn only to find that the jobs I was most interested in had attracted over a hundred applicants within just two hours of being posted. Meanwhile, my severance was dwindling rapidly.

I realized I needed to look inward and ask myself some hard questions. Was there something wrong with me for not fitting into the mold of a specialist? Why did I feel compelled to pursue so many different passions, even when it seemed to put me at a disadvantage? Exploring these thoughts, I began journaling and reflecting on what truly mattered to me. In those quiet moments of introspection, I started to understand that my so-called disadvantages were my greatest assets. I began to see the value in owning my plurality—embracing and truly appreciating the breadth of my interests and talents. It dawned on me that this diversity wasn't something to downplay or apologize for but something to celebrate. By fully embracing all the different facets of who I was, I could live a more authentic and fulfilling life. I could leverage my unique combination of skills and passions, not only to create a career that suited me but also to find success and satisfaction on my own terms. It became clear that the key to my happiness wasn't in narrowing my focus to fit the mold but in embracing the full spectrum of who I was. Owning my plurality meant giving myself permission to explore, to experiment, and to pursue a variety of paths without guilt or hesitation. And in doing so, I discovered a newfound confidence in my ability to navigate my career, not as a specialist, but as someone who thrives in the richness of multiple passions. Could it really be that simple? Was it just a matter of deciding to unapologetically embrace who I am? If I did this, would the fear that no employer would value my broad experience fade away? Would I gain the confidence to articulate my collective experiences as the superpower they truly are?

As it turned out, it was that simple. By giving myself permission to embrace more than one why I liberated myself. The temptation to reduce my diverse interests and background to a single motivating force risked oversimplifying my life, merely applying a new version of the specialist ideal to myself. Instead, embracing my complexity—acknowledging myself as a nuanced being full of contradictions and surprises—was incredibly freeing. I was finally *owning* it!

To increase psychological ownership of your nonlinear career path, focus on five key strategies that will build confidence and empower you to embrace your unique journey.

- Regularly acknowledge and celebrate your achievements, no matter how small. Reflect on your unique journey and document your successes to provide a tangible reminder of

the value you bring to your roles. This practice reinforces your confidence and helps combat self-doubt.
- Cultivate a positive mindset by practicing positive self-talk. When self-doubt arises, consciously reframe your thoughts to focus on your strengths and past successes. Develop affirmations like "I am adaptable and thrive in new environments" to reinforce your self-esteem and confidence.
- Rehearse your career narrative until it becomes second nature. Craft a story that highlights the common threads in your diverse experiences, such as problem-solving or leadership, and practice telling it confidently. Seek feedback from trusted mentors or colleagues to refine your narrative and ensure it effectively communicates your unique strengths.
- Leverage the power of visualization to mentally prepare for challenging situations. Visualize yourself navigating interviews or presentations with confidence and set positive intentions before important career moments. This mental rehearsal can help focus your mind and reinforce your self-assurance.
- Gather support and feedback from a trusted network. Regularly connect with mentors or peers who can provide encouragement and help you see your strengths more clearly. Through engaging with a supportive community, you can reinforce your confidence and provide new perspectives on your career journey.

By integrating these strategies—acknowledging achievements, practicing positive self-talk, crafting your narrative, visualizing success, and seeking support—you can take greater ownership of your nonlinear career path, turning perceived weaknesses into unique strengths.

As you fully embrace and own your nonlinear career path, recognizing the unique strengths and perspectives it brings, the next step is to deepen this sense of ownership by embodying the future you envision. Owning your journey is only the beginning; now it's time to step into the version of yourself that you aspire to become. By cultivating the feeling state of who you want to be you can begin to live as if your aspirations are already reality, and it all starts with aligning your thoughts, actions, and emotions to your desired future self, helping you to not only see yourself as capable but to feel and act as the accomplished professional you are becoming.

CHAPTER 6

FEEL IT

Assume you are what you want to be. Walk in that assumption and it will harden into fact.
—*Neville Goddard,* Feeling Is the Secret

Imagine stepping into a future where you embody the person you've always aspired to be—where your career reflects your deepest desires and truest potential. This isn't just a dream; it's a reality you can create by aligning with your future self and feeling into the experiences you wish to manifest. This chapter will guide you on a journey to explore what it means to connect with your future self and provide practices to cultivate the feeling state that will lead you to your richest, most fulfilling career.

The Power of Feeling into Your Future

Neville Goddard, a pioneering thinker in the realm of self-actualization, once said, "Assume you are what you want to be. Walk in that assumption and it will harden into fact."[10] The essence of this quote lies in the power of feeling—embracing the emotions associated

---

[10] Neville Goddard, *Feeling Is the Secret* (CreateSpace Independent Publishing Platform, 2015), 33.

with the life you want to create. This emotional alignment is not just a motivational tool; it's the key to transforming your dreams into reality.

When you allow yourself to fully feel what it would be like to live your ideal career, you're not just imagining success—you're creating a blueprint that your subconscious mind will follow. This process requires you to step into a future version of yourself and act as if you've already achieved your goals. The more vividly you can feel into this future, the more likely you are to bring it into your present reality.

The Journey Begins: Practices to Embody Your Future Self

To truly feel into your future self, you must engage in practices that elevate your state of being and connect you with the emotions of your desired career path. Use these strategies to help you on this journey:

Gratitude as a Gateway to Higher Consciousness

Gratitude is a powerful practice that can elevate your consciousness and transform your internal state. By regularly expressing gratitude, you can shift your focus from what you lack to what you have, fostering a positive outlook that aligns with the future you wish to create. Start a gratitude journal where you document not only what you're grateful for today but also the things you will be grateful for in your future career. This practice reinforces the belief that your future self is already on its way to you.

Visualize Your Future

Visualization is a potent tool for manifesting your future. Take time each day to close your eyes and imagine yourself living the career you desire. Picture yourself in your ideal work environment, interacting with colleagues who respect and value you, and achieving the milestones that are important to you. The more detailed your visualization, the stronger the emotional connection you'll build with your future self.

Example Exercise

Find a quiet space and sit comfortably. Close your eyes and take a few deep breaths to center yourself. Begin to visualize your future career in vivid detail. See yourself in the role you desire, feeling confident, accomplished, and fulfilled. As you visualize, pay attention to how this future version of you feels. Is there a sense of peace, excitement, or satisfaction? Allow these emotions to wash over you, deepening your connection to this future reality.

Spend at least ten minutes in this visualization, allowing yourself to fully embody the feelings of your future self.

Practice Mindfulness and Presence

Mindfulness is the practice of being fully present in the moment, which is essential for connecting with your future self. When you're mindful, you can more easily recognize the opportunities and experiences that align with your future goals. Incorporate mindfulness practices such as meditation, deep breathing, or mindful walking into your daily routine to enhance your awareness and presence.

Seek Feedback for Growth

Feedback is an essential component of personal and professional growth. Regularly seeking feedback from others can help you uncover blind spots and identify areas for improvement, making it easier to align with your future self. Whether it's constructive criticism or praise, feedback helps you understand how others perceive you and how you can adjust your actions to better reflect the person you want to become.

Example Exercise

Choose one person you trust and respect and ask them for specific feedback on your performance or behavior.

Reflect on the feedback you receive, considering how it aligns with your vision of your future self.

Use the feedback to create an actionable plan for growth, focusing on areas where you can improve or amplify your strengths.

Embrace Emotional Resilience

On your journey to becoming your future self, you will encounter challenges and setbacks. Building emotional resilience is key to navigating these obstacles with grace and composure. Practice self-compassion and remind yourself that growth is nonlinear—there will be ups and downs, but each experience is a valuable part of your journey.

Example Exercise

When faced with a challenge, take a moment to pause and acknowledge your feelings without judgment.

Reflect on how your future self would handle this situation. What strengths or insights would future you draw upon?

Use this reflection to guide your response, choosing actions that align with your future self's wisdom and resilience.

As you continue to cultivate the feeling state that aligns with your future self, you'll begin to notice how these internal shifts influence not only your actions but also how you perceive and navigate your career path. This nonlinear journey, with all its twists, turns, and unexpected opportunities, becomes clearer as you learn to trust your inner guidance. Yet, as important as it is to feel into your future, it's equally vital to communicate this evolving vision to others. The next step in your journey involves articulating your nonlinear career path—sharing your unique story in a way that resonates with others, whether in interviews, networking conversations, or leadership discussions. How you communicate your journey will be pivotal for aligning external perceptions with your internal evolution, ensuring that others see the value and direction of your unconventional career trajectory.

CHAPTER 7

COMMUNICATE IT

Communication works for those who work at it.
—John Powell, *Why Am I Afraid to Tell You Who I Am?*

I used to think I could just wing it, but now I know that confidently communicating my story and selling myself comes from intentional preparation and practice.

Navigating the twists and turns of a nonlinear career path can feel like an overwhelming journey, especially when you are faced with unexpected setbacks like job loss. However, these challenges can become the very catalyst needed to redefine and communicate your professional brand. To effectively convey your diverse career experiences, resilience, and adaptability to potential employers, you need to use the art of storytelling. Whether you're reentering the job market or looking to pivot to a new industry, understanding how to narrate your career journey is essential.

Embrace the Catalyst as an Opportunity

For me and many others, the catalyst for finding new ways to communicate my professional brand came in the form of the devastating experience of losing a job. I felt like a part of me had been ripped away without my permission. My confidence took a huge blow, my daily routine was incredibly disrupted, and the sudden shift in my professional identity left me filled with anxiety and fear. Along with all that, I was confronted with the harsh reality of having to start over in more ways than one. Job shopping, interviewing, learning a new company and role, building up my performance and reputational currency, forming new relationships, establishing myself as a credible thought partner—the list goes on. But amid the fear and uncertainty, I found a powerful catalyst for change. Job loss forced me to reflect deeply on my career, my skills, and my professional brand.

The initial shock of losing a job is paralyzing. I remember the day I received the news; it felt like the ground had been pulled out from under me. The questions started swirling: Would anyone else ever want to hire me? How was I going to convince someone else of my professional value? These questions poisoned my mind with doubt. But they also ignited a determination within me to overcome this setback and write my own narrative. The fear of unemployment can be transformed into motivation. It compels you to take stock of your skills, experiences, and achievements. It pushes you to refine your personal brand and prepare for the next opportunity because, unless you are financially free, you likely don't have another choice (and wouldn't be reading this book).

If that wasn't you, what was your catalyst and how can you better view it as an opportunity to better communicate your brand?

The Power of Storytelling

One of the most effective ways to communicate your nonlinear career pathway is through storytelling. Humans are wired to respond to stories; they are engaging, memorable, and relatable. By narrating your career journey as a story, you can highlight pivotal moments, challenges overcome, and lessons learned in a compelling way.

A career narrative and storytelling share similarities in that both use a narrative structure to convey information, but they serve different purposes and are employed in different contexts. A career narrative is a more strategic, focused presentation of your career journey, while storytelling, particularly in the context of career development, involves using creative techniques to make your journey engaging, relatable, and memorable. They differ in these key ways:

Purpose and focus:

The primary purpose of a career narrative is to communicate your professional identity and trajectory in a way that aligns with your career goals. It is often used in more formal settings, such as job applications, interviews, or professional portfolios, where clarity and relevance are key. Since it emphasizes key achievements, skills, and transitions, presenting a cohesive picture of your professional development, it is typically objective, with a strong focus on outcomes and professional growth.

On the other hand, storytelling about your career allows for more creativity and personal expression. While it still highlights your professional journey, it focuses on engaging the audience by weaving together personal anecdotes, challenges, and emotional experiences. Storytelling connects the dots between your experiences in a way that is memorable, often making it more effective in informal settings, like networking events or personal blogs, where the goal is to connect emotionally with your audience.

Structure and style:

A career narrative is structured around clear, logical progression, highlighting the most relevant aspects of your career that align with your desired direction. It is more concise, often resembling a summary or report, and is framed around key milestones, skill sets, and achievements. The language is typically formal and targeted, ensuring that the narrative directly relates to your professional objectives, whether that's a new role, a promotion, or career transition.

Storytelling, in contrast, is more fluid and may not always follow a linear path. It allows for flexibility in how you present your experiences—sometimes focusing more on the lessons learned or personal transformations rather than strictly adhering to chronological order. Storytelling tends to use more descriptive, emotive language, drawing on imagery and metaphors to make the content relatable and engaging for the audience. It invites the audience to empathize with your journey, making it less formal and more conversational.

Tone and audience:

The tone of a career narrative is generally professional and factual, aimed at impressing potential employers or collaborators. It prioritizes what is most relevant to your career aspirations and often omits personal struggles or detours that are less directly related to professional success. The goal is to present yourself as a capable, adaptable professional whose experiences are directly applicable to future roles.

In storytelling, the tone can be more personal and reflective, allowing for vulnerability and honesty about the ups and downs of your career. It's less about creating a perfect picture and more about sharing relatable experiences that resonate emotionally with the audience. In this way, storytelling can build rapport and connection by showing the human side of your career, making it more suitable for settings where personal connection is the priority.

Keeping these differences in mind, craft an effective career story, using your outputs from the previous chapters where you identified the key themes and moments in your professional journey. What experiences have shaped you? What challenges have you overcome? What accomplishments are you most proud of? These elements form the foundation of your narrative.

Next, highlight ***pivotal moments***. Pivotal moments are the turning points in your career. They are the experiences that have significantly impacted your professional growth and direction. For example, when I transitioned from a technical role to a business-facing role, then to a managerial position, each was a significant shift that challenged me to develop new skills and perspectives. Highlighting such moments shows your ability to adapt and grow.

Every career has its share of ***challenges***. These obstacles, whether they are difficult projects, interpersonal conflicts, or job loss, demonstrate your resilience and problem-solving abilities. By sharing how you overcame these challenges, you can showcase your strength and determination.

Lessons learned are the takeaways from your experiences. They reflect your growth and maturity as a professional. For instance, losing my job taught me the importance of continuous learning and staying adaptable. It also reinforced the value of networking and maintaining strong professional relationships.

Develop Structural Clarity

Effectively communicating your career story, especially in the context of a nonlinear career path, requires more than just identifying key moments. It involves weaving these moments into a coherent narrative that not only resonates with your audience but also aligns with your current career goals and future aspirations. For individuals with diverse experiences across various fields or industries, structuring your career story can be particularly challenging. However, with a thoughtful approach, you can turn this complexity into a compelling narrative that highlights your unique strengths and versatility. A well-structured story has a clear beginning, middle, and end, despite the twists and turns along the way. The key is to connect these parts in a way that makes sense to your audience and positions you as a strong candidate or thought leader in your chosen field.

Beginning: Setting the Stage

The beginning of your story is your opportunity to introduce yourself and set the context for your career journey. For those with nonlinear paths, this introduction is crucial. Start by framing your diverse experiences as a series of intentional choices, even if they weren't immediately connected. Highlight your educational background, early career choices, and any significant influences or motivations that led you to explore various fields. These could include personal passions, market trends, or key mentors who encouraged you to pursue different opportunities.

You might say: "My career began in [field/industry], where I honed my skills in [specific area]. However, my curiosity and drive for innovation led me to explore [different field/industry], where I gained valuable insights and new competencies." By setting the stage this way, you demonstrate that your nonlinear path was not random but driven by a desire to broaden your skillset and perspectives.

Middle: The Journey

The middle of your story is where you delve into the heart of your career journey—this is where the richness of a nonlinear path truly shines. Focus on the pivotal moments, challenges, and transitions that define your professional evolution. This section is about showing how your varied experiences have shaped your adaptability, resilience, and ability to learn quickly. Be specific about the skills you've acquired and how they've been transferable across different roles or industries.

Consider discussing how a challenge taught you problem-solving skills that you later applied in a completely different context. Use concrete examples to illustrate how these diverse experiences have given you a unique perspective and a versatile skill set that sets you apart from others who may have followed a more traditional career trajectory. You could say: "While transitioning from [industry A] to [industry B], I encountered significant challenges in [specific area].

However, this experience taught me the importance of [key skill], which I later applied successfully in [another role/industry]."

End: Reflection and Future Aspirations

The end of your story should provide a thoughtful reflection of your journey, tying together the various threads of your career and outlining your aspirations for the future. For those with nonlinear career paths, this is where you can emphasize the value of your diverse background. Reflect on how your unique journey has prepared you for the next chapter of your career and how it aligns with your long-term goals. Discuss how your varied experiences have given you a broad perspective and the ability to approach problems from different angles. Highlight your commitment to continuous learning and growth, and how this mindset will drive your future success. This is also the time to articulate your career goals, whether it's advancing in your current field, pivoting to a new industry, or taking on leadership roles that leverage your wide-ranging experience.

You might conclude with: "Looking ahead, I am eager to leverage my diverse experiences to [specific future goal]. My journey has equipped me with [specific skills or perspectives], which I believe will be invaluable as I pursue [career aspiration]."

My Personal Example

I'm Kristin Jemison and I'm a global business operations specialist. One of my first jobs, if you put aside babysitting, was working as a second-shift janitor in a PepsiCo manufacturing plant. That role taught me the value of an education and that with the right education and a little tenacity, I could be whatever I wanted.

I earned a degree in general science and started my career with Bristol Myers Squibb as a lab technician in biologics manufacturing. Over my tenure with the company, I had roles ranging from very technical roles as a scientist to general management roles leading a brand and a business unit. The common thread among all the roles I've had is that each provided me with the opportunity to create a unique solution to a complex business challenge and gave me a greater appreciation of the holistic business by understanding its parts.

This diverse breadth of experience is my superpower. I'm able to relate to different types of people and help them relate to one another by translating between them. I'm a bridge builder who loves working with interdisciplinary teams, connecting the dots across functions, and driving enterprise value.

My ten-year career goal is to be a chief operating officer in the life sciences industry. This role would provide exposure to operational leadership experiences and cost-effective strategies that align with the strategic and operational aspects of that role.

Enhance Delivery and Engagement

The way you deliver your story is just as important as its content. Practicing storytelling helps you improve your delivery techniques, making your stories more engaging and impactful. This includes:

<u>Use Vocal Variety</u>

Vocal variety is a powerful tool in storytelling. It involves changing your tone, pitch, and pace to make your narrative more dynamic and engaging. Vocal variety—tone, pitch, and pace—can enhance your storytelling.

Tone

Your tone sets the emotional atmosphere of your story. By varying your tone, you can convey different emotions, such as excitement, sadness, or suspense. Practicing helps you become more aware of how your tone influences your audience's perception of and reaction to your story. For instance, a warm, enthusiastic tone can draw your audience in and make them more receptive, while a calm, serious tone can underscore the gravity of a particular point.

Pitch

The pitch of your voice can add emphasis and highlight important parts of your story. A higher pitch can express excitement or urgency, while a lower pitch can convey seriousness or authority. Regular practice allows you to modulate your pitch effectivelyw, ensuring your story remains interesting and keeps your audience's attention.

Pace

The speed at which you speak can significantly impact your storytelling. Speaking too quickly can make it hard for your audience to follow your story, while speaking too slowly can make it drag. Practicing different pacing techniques helps you find a natural rhythm that enhances your story's flow. For example, you can speed up during exciting parts to build intensity and slow down during important moments to allow the audience to absorb the information.

Incorporate Body Language

Body language—gestures, facial expressions, and posture—plays an important role in storytelling. It helps convey emotions, illustrate points, and engage your audience.

Gestures

Gestures can help illustrate your story and make abstract concepts more tangible. Practicing different gestures can help you find ones that feel natural and effectively complement your narrative. For example, using hand movements to mimic actions in your story can make your descriptions more vivid and relatable.

Facial Expressions

Your facial expressions can convey a wide range of emotions, from joy and surprise to sadness and frustration. Practicing in front of a mirror or recording yourself can help you become more aware of your facial expressions and ensure they match the emotions you're trying to convey. This alignment between your words and expressions can make your storytelling more authentic and impactful.

Posture

Your posture can communicate confidence and openness or nervousness and defensiveness. Practicing good posture, such as standing or sitting up straight, can help you project confidence and engage your audience more effectively. Additionally, leaning slightly forward can show interest and engagement, making your audience feel more connected to your story.

Maintain Eye Contact

Maintaining eye contact with your audience is a vital aspect of effective storytelling. It helps build a connection, show confidence, and keep your audience engaged.

Build Connection

Eye contact helps establish a personal connection with your audience. It makes them feel seen and included in your story. Practicing eye contact with different people, whether in small groups or larger audiences, can help you become more comfortable and natural in maintaining this connection.

Show Confidence

Making eye contact demonstrates confidence and credibility. It shows that you are comfortable with your story and your audience. Practicing in front of a mirror or with a friend can help you build this confidence. Over time, you'll become more at ease with looking your audience in the eye, which can enhance your overall presence.

Engage Your Audience

Eye contact can also help you gauge your audience's reaction and adjust your storytelling accordingly. If you notice that your audience seems disengaged or confused, you can modify your delivery to recapture their attention. Practicing eye contact allows you to become more attuned to these cues and respond effectively.

Practical Tips for Enhancing Delivery and Engagement

Use these practical tips to help you enhance your delivery and engagement through vocal variety, body language, and eye contact.

Tip 1. Record and review:

Recording yourself while practicing storytelling allows you to review your performance and identify areas for improvement. Pay attention to your vocal variety, body language, and eye contact. Note any parts where you could use more vocal variation, gestures, or more consistent eye contact.

Tip 2. Practice with a mirror:

Practicing in front of a mirror helps you observe your facial expressions and body language in real time. This exercise allows you to make immediate adjustments and become more aware of how you come across to your audience.

Tip 3. Participate in public speaking groups:

Joining public speaking groups like Toastmasters can provide you with opportunities to practice and receive constructive feedback. These groups often offer a supportive environment where you can experiment with different storytelling techniques and refine your skills.

Tip 4. Use storytelling techniques in daily conversations:

Incorporating storytelling techniques into your everyday conversations can help you practice in a low-stakes environment. Whether you're sharing an anecdote with a friend or explaining a concept at work, focus on using vocal variety, paying attention to body language, and maintaining eye contact.

Tip 5. Seek feedback:

Seeking feedback from trusted peers or mentors can provide valuable insights into your storytelling delivery. Ask them to focus on your vocal variety, body language, and eye contact, and to provide specific suggestions for improvement.

Enhancing your delivery and engagement through practice is critical for effective storytelling. By focusing on these elements, you can make your stories more dynamic, relatable, and impactful. Regular practice not only improves these specific skills but also builds your overall confidence as a storyteller. Remember, storytelling is an art that can be continuously refined. By dedicating time and effort to practice, you can become a more engaging and persuasive storyteller, capable of captivating any audience.

CHAPTER 8

THE POWER OF NETWORKING

The successful networkers I know, the ones receiving tons of referrals and feeling truly happy about themselves, continually put the other person's needs ahead of their own.
—Bob Burg, Endless Referrals

In the fast-paced and ever-evolving landscape of today's business world, the adage "It's not what you know, but who you know" holds more truth than ever before. Networking, the art of cultivating relationships with people who can help you achieve your personal and professional goals, has become an essential skill for anyone aiming to succeed in their career. Whether you are an entrepreneur, a corporate professional, or a freelancer, your network can be a powerful asset that opens doors to opportunities, provides valuable insights, and supports your growth and development.

The importance of networking extends beyond mere job hunting or business development. It encompasses gaining knowledge, staying abreast of industry trends, finding mentors and advisors, and building a personal brand. Effective networking can lead to collaborations, partnerships, and even lifelong friendships. Through these connections, individuals can share experiences, exchange ideas, and inspire each other to achieve greater heights.

Core of Networking

Networking is not just an art; it is also a science. Understanding the psychological and sociological aspects of human interactions can significantly enhance your networking skills. At its core, networking is about building trust and rapport with others. This involves understanding how people think, behave, and make decisions. One of the foundational theories that explains the power of networking is social capital theory, which refers to the resources and benefits individuals gain from their relationships with others and includes access to information, influence, social credentials, and emotional support. Social capital can be categorized into three types:

- **Bonding social capital:** This involves close-knit relationships with family, friends, and colleagues. These connections provide emotional support and a sense of belonging.
- **Bridging social capital:** These are more distant connections, such as acquaintances and colleagues from different departments or industries. Bridging social capital provides access to new information and diverse perspectives.
- **Linking social capital:** This type of social capital involves connections with individuals or groups in positions of power or authority. Linking social capital can open doors to opportunities and resources that may otherwise be inaccessible.

The Strength of Weak Ties

Another important concept in networking, introduced by sociologist Mark Granovetter, is the strength of weak ties. Granovetter's research suggests that weak ties, or acquaintances, are more valuable for accessing new information and opportunities than strong ties, or close friends. This is because weak ties connect you to different social circles and networks, exposing you to new ideas and resources that you would not encounter within your immediate circle.

Reciprocity and Altruism

Effective networking is built on the principles of reciprocity and altruism. Reciprocity refers to the practice of exchanging favors and resources with others. When you help someone, they are more likely to help you in return. Altruism, on the other hand, involves helping others without expecting anything in return. Altruistic acts can build goodwill and strengthen your network, as people are naturally inclined to reciprocate kindness and support.

The Role of Trust

Trust is a critical component of successful networking. Trustworthy individuals are seen as reliable, honest, and competent, making others more willing to engage with them and share valuable information. Building trust takes time and consistent effort. It involves being authentic, keeping promises, and demonstrating integrity in all your interactions.

Different Ways to Network

While this chapter focuses on networking online, networking can take many forms, ranging from formal events to casual conversations. Understanding the different ways to network can help you choose the methods that best suit your personality, goals, and industry.

Network in Person

- **Professional conferences and seminars:** These events provide opportunities to meet industry leaders, learn about the latest trends, and connect with peers.

- **Networking events:** Many organizations host networking events specifically designed to facilitate connections among professionals.
- **Workshops and training sessions:** Participating in workshops and training sessions can help you build skills while expanding your network.
- **Informal meetups:** Casual gatherings, such as coffee meetings or social events, can be an effective way to build relationships in a relaxed setting.

Network Online

- **Social media platforms:** Sites like LinkedIn, X, and Facebook offer opportunities to connect with professionals worldwide.
- **Online forums and communities:** Joining industry-specific forums and online communities can help you engage in discussions and build relationships with like-minded individuals.
- **Webinars and virtual events:** Virtual events and webinars provide opportunities to learn and network with professionals from the comfort of your home or office.
- **Email and messaging:** Personalized emails and direct messages can be a powerful way to connect with individuals and build relationships.

Leverage Existing Connections

- **Referrals and introductions:** Asking your existing contacts for referrals or introductions can help you expand your network quickly.
- **Mentorship and sponsorship:** Building relationships with mentors and sponsors can lead to guidance, support, and access to their networks.

- **Alumni networks:** Engaging with your school or university alumni network can help you connect with professionals who share a common background.

Network Through Volunteering

- **Professional associations:** Joining professional associations and participating in their activities can help you meet industry leaders and peers.
- **Community service:** Volunteering for community service projects can help you build relationships while making a positive impact on society.
- **Nonprofit organizations:** Serving on the board of or volunteering with nonprofit organizations can expand your network and enhance your reputation.

Identify Your Personal Networking Strategy

Developing a personal networking strategy involves understanding your goals, identifying your target audience, and leveraging the right tools and methods to build meaningful connections. Use this step-by-step framework to help you create an effective networking strategy:

Step 1: Define Your Networking Goals

- **Career advancement:** Are you looking to advance in your current role or find a new job?
- **Business development:** Do you want to generate leads, find partners, or grow your business?
- **Knowledge and skill building:** Are you seeking to learn new skills, gain industry insights, or find mentors?
- **Personal growth:** Are you looking to build confidence, improve your communication skills, or expand your social circle?

Step 2: Identify Your Target Audience

- **Industry professionals:** Identify professionals in your industry or related fields who can provide valuable insights and opportunities.
- **Influencers and thought leaders:** Connect with industry influencers and thought leaders to stay updated on trends and gain exposure.
- **Peers and colleagues:** Build relationships with peers and colleagues who can provide support and collaboration opportunities.
- **Mentors and advisors:** Seek out mentors and advisors who can guide you in your career or business journey.

Step 3: Choose Your Networking Methods

- **In-person networking:** Attend conferences, seminars, and networking events. Schedule one-on-one meetings and join professional associations.
- **Online networking:** Leverage social media platforms like LinkedIn, X, and online forums. Participate in webinars and virtual events.
- **Volunteering and community engagement:** Get involved in community service projects, nonprofit organizations, and professional associations.
- **Referrals and introductions:** Ask your existing contacts for referrals and introductions to expand your network.

Step 4: Develop a Networking Plan

- **Set specific goals:** Define specific, measurable goals for your networking efforts, such as the number of new connections you want to make each month.

- **Create a schedule:** Allocate time for networking activities, such as attending events, engaging on social media, and following up with contacts.
- **Prepare your elevator pitch:** Develop a concise and compelling elevator pitch that summarizes who you are, what you do, and what you are looking for.
- **Prepare conversation starters:** Think of conversation starters and questions to ask when meeting new people. This can help ease anxiety and facilitate meaningful conversations.

Step 5: Track and Evaluate Your Progress

- **Maintain a contact list:** Keep a list of your contacts, including their roles, their industries, and how you met them. Note any follow-up actions or topics of interest.
- **Follow up regularly:** Regularly check in with your contacts to maintain relationships. Send personalized messages, share relevant content, and offer assistance.
- **Evaluate your strategy:** Periodically evaluate your networking strategy to determine what is working and what needs improvement. Adjust your approach based on feedback and results.

Step 6: Stay Authentic and Provide Value

- **Be authentic:** Be genuine and authentic in your interactions. People are more likely to connect with you if they perceive you as trustworthy and sincere.
- **Provide value:** Focus on providing value to your network. Share useful information, offer assistance, and support others in achieving their goals.
- **Be patient:** Building a strong network takes time and effort. Be patient and persistent and remember that relationships are built on trust and reciprocity.

Build Your Personal Online Presence

In today's digital era, building an online presence is not just beneficial but **_essential_** for professionals across all industries. Nothing is more expensive than a missed opportunity. If your professional online presence is minimal to nonexistent, I can assure you that you have left opportunities on the table and unexploited and will continue to do so if you do not give this area more attention. Online platforms offer the opportunity to both build and control your personal brand. Ask yourself, "What am I saying to the world?" If you are saying nothing online, that's your personal brand. If you like everything from everyone all the time, that's your personal brand. If you create drama online, that's your personal brand. And if you are intentional and focused with your engagement, you guessed it—that's your personal brand.

By consistently sharing valuable content, engaging with your target audience, and showcasing your unique strengths, you can position yourself as a thought leader and expert in your field. An active online presence facilitates networking by connecting you with peers, industry leaders, and influencers. Social media platforms and professional forums enable meaningful interactions and discussions, fostering relationships that can lead to mentorships, partnerships, and job opportunities.

Before you start engaging on any social media platform in a professional capacity, it's important to think about what you want your personal brand to be. Creating your online personal brand can be viewed as an extension of the career narrative you created in chapter 4. You will establish your online presence in a similar fashion—through introspection, organization, and strategic thinking.

The first step to take when determining your personal brand is to think about what you want your brand to be. Figure out your goals:

- What is your direction?
- Who do you want to talk to?

- Who is your audience?
- And what are your social media platforms?

Next, be clear on what you want to be known for. For example, with a goal to establish myself as a credible, multidisciplinary biopharmaceutical professional, my online engagement focuses on three distinct areas: technical operations, authentic leadership, and innovative science. Any professional online engagement—from original content I create to content and people I engage with—usually relates in some way to these three areas. It's also a good idea to post content from time to time that helps people get to know you as a person. Personal content that doesn't relate specifically to one of your distinct areas but helps your audience get to know you can be an advantage when it comes to standing out in a good way online.

Now consider your audience. Who will you engage with? Your target audience will dictate how you communicate, so get to know the community of people in the space. Connect with them, pay attention to their responses and feedback, and be an influencer in their areas of interest. As part of my research for writing this book, I polled my audience on LinkedIn about which personal branding topics would interest them the most. How to more effectively communicate your personal brand was the overwhelming winner, which is why the chapter on communication is one of the most robust.

Create your personal mission statement. Use your career narrative as a starting point. Look at the collective experiences you have chosen to highlight and bring forward. Pull out the key themes and focus on the strengths that demonstrate your plurality and multidimensionality. Roll these up into a concise statement you feel fits you.

Example:

> I'm Kristin Jemison, and I'm a business operations executive.

I enhance patients' lives by optimizing the way matrixed teams work to bring added-value medicines to market.

Now it's time to build your online brand.

Key Considerations When Building an Online Presence

Consistency

My professional platform of choice is LinkedIn, and for the time being, I have consciously chosen to only focus there. If you choose to be on multiple platforms, maintaining a consistent online presence across them is critical. This includes using the same professional photo, bio, and contact information. Consistency helps in building a recognizable personal brand and ensures that your professional identity is coherent.

Content Quality

The quality of content shared online plays a significant role in shaping your professional image. Focus on sharing well-researched, insightful, and relevant content that adds value to your audience. To maintain credibility, avoid controversial or unprofessional topics.

Engagement

Active engagement with your online community is key to building a strong presence. This involves commenting on others' posts, joining relevant groups, participating in discussions, and responding to comments and messages. Engagement helps you build relationships and expand your network.

Privacy and Professionalism

Balancing personal and professional content is important. As a professional, be mindful of your privacy settings and the types of personal information you share. Ensuring that all publicly visible content aligns with your professional image is critical to maintaining professionalism.

Regular Updates

Regularly updating profiles and content keeps your online presence fresh and relevant. This includes posting about recent projects, achievements, and new skills. Regular updates demonstrate that you are active and continuously evolving in your career.

Building an online presence offers numerous benefits for enhancing your personal brand and networking opportunities. However, it requires careful consideration of consistency, content quality, and engagement. By strategically managing your online presence, you can leverage the digital world to advance your career and achieve your professional goals.

Picking Your Platform

Which platforms should you use to engage with your target audience and grow your career? The answer ultimately depends on your own personal goals and industry. For most, including myself, LinkedIn is the professional networking platform of choice. With over 700 million members worldwide, it provides a platform to connect with professionals across industries and geographies.

Pros and Cons of Other Professional Networking Platforms

While LinkedIn is often the default choice, several other platforms can be valuable, depending on your industry and networking goals.

X (formerly Twitter)

Pros: Great for real-time engagement, thought leadership, and following industry trends. It allows for easy interaction with influencers, industry experts, and peers through quick updates and discussions. Hashtags make it easy to follow niche topics or events.

Cons: Limited to short-form content, which can make it hard to build deep professional connections. It can be noisy, with personal and professional content often blending together, which may dilute your brand.

Meetup

Pros: Ideal for in-person networking and community building, especially if you want to connect with professionals locally. It's a great tool for attending and organizing industry-related events, workshops, and meetups.

Cons: Limited online interaction, so it's better for those looking to focus on building local or event-based connections rather than ongoing digital networking.

Slack

Pros: Often used internally within organizations, but many industries and professional groups have adopted Slack as a way to form online communities. It's highly collaborative, allowing for instant communication and knowledge sharing in specialized channels.

Cons: Requires an invitation to join most communities, so it may be harder to break into established groups. It's not as visible or searchable as other platforms for personal branding.

Facebook groups

Pros: Provides large and engaged communities around specific industries, interests, or career development topics. Groups often have focused conversations, and some can be highly active and supportive.

Cons: As Facebook is a primarily social platform, it may be hard to separate personal and professional content. Its professional relevance is also somewhat limited, as it lacks the formal tone and features of LinkedIn.

GitHub (for developers)

Pros: Excellent for building a professional portfolio for developers, showcasing work, and connecting with other developers or recruiters. GitHub provides a concrete way to demonstrate technical skills.

Cons: It's highly industry-specific, so it's not useful outside of technical fields like software development.

Each of these platforms offers its own unique set of advantages and limitations. Often the best approach is to choose one or two platforms that align closely with your professional goals and industry, ensuring you can maintain an active and effective presence.

Using LinkedIn to Elevate Yourself and Your Networking

Use these strategies to maximize your personal presence and networking efforts on LinkedIn.

Create a Strong Profile

- **Professional photo:** Use a high-quality, professional photo that represents your personal brand.
- **Compelling headline:** Write a headline that clearly communicates your expertise and value proposition.
- **Detailed summary:** Craft a summary that highlights your skills, experience, and career goals. Use keywords relevant to your industry to enhance your profile's visibility.
- **Experience and education:** Provide detailed information about your work experience and educational background. Highlight your achievements and contributions.
- **Skills and endorsements:** List your key skills and ask your connections to endorse them. Endorse others in return to build goodwill.
- **Recommendations:** Request recommendations from colleagues, supervisors, and clients. Recommendations add credibility to your profile.

Build Your Network

- **Connect with colleagues and classmates:** Start by connecting with people you know, such as colleagues, classmates, and friends.
- **Expand your network:** Use LinkedIn's search feature to find and connect with professionals in your industry. I highly recommend investing in a LinkedIn Premium membership if you are invested in building your network. This membership level enables you to personalize your connection requests to increase the likelihood of acceptance.
- **Join LinkedIn groups:** Participate in LinkedIn groups related to your industry or interests. Engage in discussions and connect with group members.

- **Engage with content:** Like, comment on, and share posts from your connections and industry leaders. This increases your visibility and helps you build relationships.

Share Valuable Content

- **Post regularly:** Share articles, insights, and updates related to your industry. This positions you as a thought leader and keeps you on the radar of people in your network.
- **Write articles:** Publish articles on LinkedIn to showcase your expertise and share your perspectives on industry trends and challenges.
- **Share achievements:** Celebrate your achievements and milestones. This can include promotions, certifications, or successful projects.

Reach Out to New Connections

- **Personalized messages:** When reaching out to new connections, send personalized messages that explain why you want to connect and how you can add value.
- **Follow up:** After connecting with someone, follow up with a message to start a conversation. This can involve discussing common interests, sharing insights, or offering assistance.
- **Maintain relationships:** Stay in touch with your connections by periodically checking in, sharing relevant content, or congratulating them on their achievements.

Networking is a powerful tool that can significantly impact your career and business success. By understanding the science behind networking, leveraging various methods to connect with others, and using platforms like LinkedIn effectively, you can build a strong and valuable network. Developing a personal networking strategy tailored to your goals and target audience will help you navigate the complexities of the modern business world and achieve your objectives. Remember, networking is not just about what others can do for you, but also about what you can do for others. Approach it with authenticity, generosity, and a willingness to learn and grow, and you will reap the rewards of a robust and supportive network.

CHAPTER 9

THE ART OF RECEIVING

Gracious acceptance is an art—
an art which most never bother to cultivate.
—*Alexander McCall Smith,* Love Over Scotland

Receiving help from others is an often overlooked but essential component of personal and professional growth. In a society that frequently glorifies self-reliance and individual achievement, the concept of asking for and accepting help can seem contrary to the ideals of independence and strength. Many of us are conditioned to believe that we must forge our own paths, solve our own problems, and achieve success on our own terms. However, this mindset can be both limiting and isolating.

The psychology behind resisting help is complex and deeply rooted. At its core, it involves a blend of pride, fear, and a desire for control. Pride can make us reluctant to show vulnerability or admit that we cannot do everything on our own. Fear plays a role as well: we fear being judged, appearing weak, or feeling indebted to others. Moreover, accepting help requires relinquishing a degree of control, which can be uncomfortable for those accustomed to managing every aspect of their lives.

However, the act of gracious acceptance is an art that few master. It requires humility, openness, and a willingness to acknowledge our limitations. Embracing help from others does not diminish our abilities or achievements; it enhances them by allowing us to leverage the strengths and experiences of those around us. When we accept help with gratitude and grace, we not only benefit from the assistance itself but also build stronger, more meaningful connections with others.

How to Make the Most of Receiving Through Networking

In the corporate world, career progression is often visualized as a linear path: starting at an entry-level position, advancing to midlevel roles, and eventually reaching senior management. However, the modern workforce increasingly recognizes that careers are not always linear. Instead, they can be nonlinear, characterized by lateral moves, industry changes, role shifts, and varied skill development. In this context, the art of receiving—being open to feedback, mentorship, opportunities, and even criticism—becomes essential to navigating and progressing along this nonlinear career trajectory.

Leverage Existing Networks

Leverage your existing network to explore new opportunities and gather insights. Reconnect with former colleagues, attend alumni events, and reach out to acquaintances in your field. These connections often lead to unexpected opportunities and provide a wealth of information about potential career paths.

Listen to Feedback

One of the most critical aspects of the art of receiving is the ability to accept and act on feedback. In a nonlinear career, where roles and industries may change, feedback serves as a guide. Constructive feedback helps us understand our strengths and areas for improvement, which is essential when transitioning between roles that require different skill sets. For instance, a marketing professional moving into a product management role must be receptive to feedback to adapt and grow in the new domain. Feedback also fosters continuous learning, which is indispensable for maintaining relevance in diverse roles.

Seek Mentorship and Guidance

Receiving mentorship is another vital component of nonlinear careers, where traditional paths and clear promotional ladders are often absent. Mentors provide invaluable insights, advice, and support, helping us navigate the complexities of career changes. They can offer perspectives that we may not have considered, identify potential opportunities, and help us avoid common pitfalls. Moreover, mentors can introduce mentees to new networks and resources, which are critical in nonlinear career paths because success relies on adaptability and connections across different industries.

Embrace Opportunities

The art of receiving also involves recognizing and seizing opportunities that may not initially align with our perceived career path. Nonlinear careers often involve detours or lateral moves that might seem counterintuitive but ultimately lead to personal and professional growth. Being open to such opportunities requires a mindset shift—seeing them not as distractions but as valuable experiences that can broaden skillsets and enhance career prospects. For instance, accepting a short-term project in a different department or even an entirely different industry can expose us to new ideas and methods, enriching our overall career journey.

Learn from Criticism

Unlike feedback, which is typically constructive, criticism can sometimes be harsh or unexpected. However, developing the resilience to absorb and reflect on criticism can lead to profound personal and professional growth. It can push us out of our comfort zones, encouraging us to develop new skills or approaches that we might not have pursued otherwise. In a nonlinear career, where change and adaptability are constants, the ability to take criticism in stride and use it as a learning tool is invaluable.

The power of receiving help from others is transformative. And it extends beyond internal and company-bound mentoring programs to building a robust network of external advisors and mentors. We will discuss the strategies for finding and connecting with the right people and how to cultivate a mindset that welcomes support and guidance. By embracing the art of receiving help, we can unlock new opportunities for growth and success, enriching our personal and professional lives in profound ways.

The Need for an External Perspective

Losing my job was a turning point. The sudden upheaval made me realize how heavily I had relied on an internal network that, while supportive, was also limited. I found myself in need of guidance from individuals who could offer an objective, external perspective on my career and personal development. I needed a network of people whose sole measure of success was my success.

Mentors: This realization led me to seek out mentors and advisors outside of any single organization. I needed people who could see my career objectively, stand outside the situations I was in, and provide honest, unbiased feedback. These individuals helped me identify where I was getting in my own way, showed me where I was closer to my goals than I had thought, and shared their hard-earned lessons on advancing a career with integrity. Their perspectives were invaluable, offering insights that were not clouded by internal politics or corporate agendas.

Career coach: Finding the right career coach is a nuanced process that requires both self-reflection and external research. It's not just about finding someone with the right qualifications; it's about finding someone who genuinely understands your unique career trajectory and nonlinear path. I started by clarifying my own goals, strengths, and areas of uncertainty, which gave me a clearer idea of what I needed in a coach. I then explored coaches with diverse specialties—some focused on career transitions, others on personal branding, and some on leadership development. It was crucial to engage with coaches who were experienced in guiding professionals through unconventional career paths, as they could offer insights and strategies that resonated with my journey. I attended their free webinars, engaged in online forums where they were active, and even reached out to former clients to gauge their experiences. This comprehensive approach ensured that when I finally chose a coach, it was someone who could truly understand my aspirations and challenges. Their guidance not only helped refine my career strategy but also instilled confidence and clarity into my decisions, making them an invaluable part of my support system.

Commit to Continued Development

In a nonlinear career path, continuous development isn't just a recommendation; it's a necessity. As industries evolve and career trajectories become less predictable, staying adaptable through constant learning is key to maintaining relevance. My approach to continued development involved creating a structured learning plan that was both flexible and comprehensive. I started by identifying the core skills and knowledge areas that were essential for my current role and future aspirations. Then I sought out the best resources—whether through formal education, industry-specific training, or self-directed learning. Accelerator programs played a significant role by providing immersive, fast-paced learning environments that pushed me out of my comfort zone and accelerated my growth. Beyond formal programs, I made it a habit to regularly consume content from thought leaders in my field, such as attending live Q&A sessions with experts or joining mastermind groups. This diverse mix of learning activities ensured that I stayed ahead of industry trends while also fostering a growth mindset that kept me open to new opportunities and challenges.

Form a Personal Board of Directors

Creating a personal board of directors was a transformative step in navigating my nonlinear career. Unlike a mentor, who typically offers advice in a more informal or general context, my board members were carefully chosen advisors who brought distinct, strategic value to my career development. I selected individuals based on their expertise, willingness to provide honest feedback, and their ability to offer different perspectives—ranging from industry-specific insights to general business acumen. These were not just colleagues but trusted advisors who understood my ambitions and the complexities of my career path. We scheduled regular meetings where I presented my progress, challenges, and upcoming decisions. These sessions were invaluable for receiving actionable advice, reality checks, and encouragement. Over time, this board became more than just a sounding board; they were a strategic asset, helping me navigate difficult decisions, capitalize on new opportunities, and stay aligned with my long-term vision. Their collective wisdom ensured that I wasn't just reacting to circumstances but proactively shaping my career path in a way that aligned with my personal and professional goals.

Action-Oriented Framework for Professional Development

Receiving help from others can be a transformative force in personal and professional growth. In a world where self-reliance is often celebrated, it's essential to recognize the power of collaboration and external support. Leveraging the insights, guidance, and expertise of mentors, coaches, and peers can accelerate your development, provide new perspectives, and help you navigate complex career landscapes.

This action-oriented framework for professional development is designed to guide you in systematically identifying areas where you need improvement, selecting focus areas, and committing to specific strategies for growth. By actively seeking and accepting help from others, you can overcome challenges more efficiently, build new skills, and achieve your career goals with greater confidence. This framework emphasizes the importance of structured planning, continuous learning, and the invaluable role of external support in achieving long-term success.

Step 1: Identify Areas for Improvement

Begin by reflecting on your professional development needs. Consider the following areas where you might seek improvement:

- **Communication**: Enhancing verbal and writing skills to convey ideas effectively.
- **Leadership**: Developing the ability to inspire and manage teams.
- **Data analysis**: Improving proficiency in interpreting and utilizing data.
- **Executive presence**: Building confidence and poise in high-stakes situations.

Step 2: Select Focus Areas

Choose a few areas to concentrate on over the next year. Document these focus areas in your personal development plan. For example, you might focus on communication and leadership.

Step 3: Commit to Improvement Strategies

For each focus area, determine a specific strategy to work toward over the next year. Consider the following examples:

Communication

- **Take on a new role**: Volunteer for a position that requires frequent public speaking or presentation.
- **Develop in current role**: Lead a team project where you will need to communicate with diverse stakeholders.
- **Employee development program**: Enroll in a company-sponsored communication skills workshop.
- **External resources**: Sign up for a public speaking course at a local community college or online.
- **Budget for development**: Allocate funds to hire a communication coach.
- **Timing and location**: Plan to attend evening classes twice a week for six months.
- **Level of help needed**: Opt for tailored coaching sessions to address specific communication challenges.

Leadership

- **Take on a new role**: Apply for a managerial position within your department.
- **Develop in current role**: Take charge of a special project that involves coordinating cross-functional teams.

- **Employee development program**: Participate in your employer's leadership development program.
- **External resources**: Attend a leadership conference or seminar.
- **Budget for development**: Set aside money for a leadership certification program.
- **Timing and location**: Join a weekend leadership boot camp scheduled quarterly.
- **Level of help needed**: Engage in a mini-class to develop foundational leadership skills.

Step 4: Implement and Track Progress

Document your commitments and track your progress regularly. Create a timeline with milestones to ensure you stay on course. For example, if communication is your focus area, you may have a timeline that looks like this:

- **January**: Enroll in a public speaking course.
- **February–April**: Attend weekly classes and practice speaking skills.
- **May**: Present a project update at a company meeting.
- **June–August**: Participate in monthly webinars on effective communication.
- **September**: Evaluate progress and seek feedback from peers.
- **October–December**: Work with a communication coach to refine advanced skills.

Step 5: Review and Adjust

At the end of the year, review your progress and achievements. Assess whether you met your development goals and identify any areas that still need improvement. Adjust your development plan as necessary for the coming year.

The art of receiving is indispensable in navigating a nonlinear career path in the corporate world. Whether it's feedback, mentorship, opportunities, or criticism, being open to external input allows us to adapt, grow, and thrive in diverse roles and industries. As careers become less about climbing a ladder and more about exploring a labyrinth of possibilities, the ability to receive—and effectively act upon—external influences becomes a critical component of sustained success. This openness not only facilitates continuous learning but also empowers us to shape our unique career journeys, making the most of the opportunities that come our way.

CHAPTER 10

POSITION IT

Position yourself accordingly to maximize your impact.
— Germany Kent

Personal positioning is a crucial aspect of career development, especially in today's dynamic job market. It involves strategically defining and presenting your unique strengths, skills, and experiences to stand out in a competitive landscape. For those of us with nonlinear career paths, personal positioning becomes even more vital. Our diverse experiences, though seemingly disconnected, can be our greatest asset if properly articulated. By carefully crafting a narrative that highlights transferable skills and unique perspectives gained from varied roles, we can effectively position ourselves as adaptable and versatile candidates, making us highly attractive to potential employers across different industries.

After I was laid off in 2023, I briefly considered leaving the industry. I had accumulated a respectable breadth of skills and experience that was marketable as transferable, so a new industry was a very real possibility. I even considered becoming my own boss and starting a business. Many of the qualities that had made me successful in my biopharma career, such as adaptability, creativity, and a healthy appetite for taking strategic risks, would be assets in business ownership. I started working with a coach who helped me evaluate whether business ownership was the right move for me, a process I was executing in parallel with researching different job industries as part of my "What is it I really want to do with my life?" journey. I knew in my heart that whatever I ended up doing had to be something aligned with my personal mission statement and that I had a passion for.

Changing Industries

Changing industries is a significant decision that requires careful thought and planning. While it can lead to new opportunities and professional growth, it also comes with risks and challenges. If you're contemplating this career move, consider the following:

Self-Assessment

Before making a move, enhance your Finding Your Whys exercise from chapter 2 by asking yourself the following questions to understand your strengths, weaknesses, interests, and values. Understanding your own professional identity and aspirations will help you make a more informed decision.

- What are my core skills and how transferable are they to the new industry?
- What are my career goals and how does this change align with them?
- What motivates me and how will this new industry fulfill these motivations?

Research the Target Industry

Gain a comprehensive understanding of the industry you want to enter. This involves:

- **Industry trends:** Research current trends, future outlooks, and potential growth areas.
- **Key players:** Identify leading companies and influential figures within the industry.
- **Typical career paths:** Understand common roles, career progression, and skill requirements.

Reading industry reports, attending relevant webinars, and following industry news can also provide valuable insights.

Skills and Qualifications

Investing time in skill development is crucial to making a successful transition. Evaluate the skills and qualifications required for the new industry. Consider:

- **Educational requirements:** Do you need additional degrees or certifications?
- **Skill gaps:** Identify any gaps in your skills and plan how to bridge them. This might involve taking courses, gaining certifications, or gaining relevant experience through volunteering or part-time work.

Networking

A strong network will be, unequivocally, the most valuable asset you have in navigating a career change, whether you decide to change industries or not. It's who you know, not what you know. Building a professional network in your new industry can provide support and open doors. Strategies include:

- **Connecting with industry professionals:** Use LinkedIn, industry events, and professional associations to meet people in the field.
- **Informational interviews:** Conduct interviews with professionals to gain insights and advice about the industry and its demands.
- **Mentorship:** Seek mentors who can guide you through the transition process and offer valuable industry-specific advice.

Financial Considerations

Changing industries can impact your financial situation. Financial planning is essential to ensure a smooth and sustainable transition. Consider:

- **Salary differences:** Research average salaries in the new industry and compare them to your current earnings.
- **Transition costs:** Account for potential costs such as additional education and training, or for temporary income reduction during the transition period.
- **Savings:** Ensure that you have a financial cushion to support you through the transition period without undue stress.

Company Culture and Work-Life Balance

Different industries can have vastly different work cultures and expectations. Aligning your personal preferences with the industry norms can significantly impact your job satisfaction and overall well-being. Reflect on:

- **Company culture:** What kind of work environment suits you best? Collaborative, competitive, structured, or flexible?
- **Work-life balance:** Understand the typical work hours, travel requirements, and remote work options in the new industry.

Long-Term Prospects

Making sure the industry offers sustainable career prospects is critical for long-term success.

Consider the new industry's long-term viability and opportunities within it:

- **Job security:** Evaluate the stability of the industry and its vulnerability to economic fluctuations.
- **Career advancement:** Assess the potential for growth and advancement in the industry.

Changing industries is a multifaceted decision that involves introspection, research, and strategic planning. You can make a more informed and confident transition by taking action on the framework discussed. Taking a thoughtful and methodical approach will increase your chances of finding success and satisfaction in your new career path.

I decided to stay in the biopharmaceutical industry for a few distinct reasons. Primarily, my compensation would be negatively impacted by a switch, which was not something I believed to be in my or my family's best interest. I also didn't feel done with biopharma. In my soul I knew I still had more to give, more patient lives to positively impact, and more room to grow professionally. Finally, I believed I would have a better chance of differentiating myself from others and positioning myself for new roles if I stayed within the industry that my professional experience and accomplishments were in. This is not to say you should not consider or take action on an industry change if you feel it is the right thing for you. I simply did not feel it was the right thing for me.

In today's dynamic job market, many professionals have nonlinear career paths. While this offers a rich tapestry of experiences, it can also pose challenges in positioning yourself effectively to future employers. This can be harder to do if you have decided to change industries, as you will be coming in with fewer industry-specific accomplishments than those with whom you are competing for roles. While it will be more difficult, nothing is impossible if you are willing to put in the work. Positioning yourself is work. Positioning is how you differentiate yourself in the mind of the prospect. That is, you position the product (*you*) in the mind of the prospect (*hiring manager*). Think like the hiring manager. Here's how you can make the most of your unique journey and present it as an asset.

A Recruiter's Perspective

While I surely recognize the value of the diverse skill set my nonlinear career path offers, I have often felt that many recruiters do not know what to make of it. Perhaps you feel the same. My experience, as well as that of others with nonlinear career paths I've consulted with, is that—regardless of the level of impact and influence we've been able to achieve—many recruiters do not know what to do with someone who has a resume like ours that ebbs and flows through a company or industry in several different roles. No matter how many times I was told by others that my breadth of experience was my superpower, it was difficult to own it when I was being ghosted by recruiters or flat-out rejected with the "we think you're amazing but we're going with someone whose experience better fits the role" automated email. As a result, for years I tried to put myself into a linear box to fit a job description, make the life of recruiters easier, and increase my chances of getting a phone screening.

To alleviate my personal frustration and educate myself, I researched how recruiters evaluate candidates with linear vs. nonlinear career pathways. I have reported my findings below. I share these with you to enhance your holistic understanding of the recruiter evaluation process because when you understand how recruiters think, you will be better positioned to strategically communicate how you exemplify the strengths of those with nonlinear career pathways and turn the stereotypical challenges into a competitive advantage.

Analyzing Recruiter Evaluations of Linear vs. Nonlinear Career Pathways

Recruiters often serve as gatekeepers to employment opportunities, evaluating a wide array of candidates to find the best fit for specific roles. The way recruiters assess candidates can vary significantly depending on whether the candidate has followed a linear or nonlinear career pathway. Understanding these differences can provide insights into the hiring process and the values that recruiters place on different career trajectories. This analysis explores the nuances in recruiter evaluations of candidates with linear and nonlinear career paths, focusing on the strengths and challenges associated with each pathway.

Linear Career Pathways

Definition and Characteristics: A linear career pathway is characterized by a clear, logical progression within a single field or industry. This type of career often includes a series of related positions that demonstrate upward mobility, such as promotions or increased responsibilities. For example, a marketing professional might start as a marketing assistant, progress to a marketing manager, and eventually become a marketing director.

Strengths in Recruiter Evaluations

- **Consistency and predictability**: Recruiters often value linear career paths for their predictability. A candidate with a linear career trajectory demonstrates a clear commitment to

a particular field, reducing the perceived risk of job-hopping or lack of direction.
- **Skill development**: Linear careers often allow for deep specialization. Recruiters can easily trace the development of relevant skills and experiences, making it simpler to match the candidate's qualifications with the job requirements.
- **Easier fit assessment**: Evaluating candidates with linear career paths is generally more straightforward. Their progression often aligns with industry standards and expectations, making it easier for recruiters to gauge their suitability for specific roles.

Challenges in Recruiter Evaluations

- **Potential for Stagnation**: While linear career paths can indicate stability, they might also suggest a lack of innovation or flexibility. Recruiters might be concerned that the candidate is too narrowly focused or resistant to change.
- **Assumption of Traditional Career Models**: Linear career paths fit traditional career models, which might not align with the evolving nature of work. This can sometimes limit the perceived adaptability of the candidate to dynamic or interdisciplinary roles.

Nonlinear Career Pathways

Definition and Characteristics: A nonlinear career pathway is marked by a diverse range of roles across different fields or industries. This type of career might include lateral moves, career changes, or periods of freelancing and entrepreneurial endeavors. For instance, a candidate might have experience in teaching, project management, and content creation.

Strengths in Recruiter Evaluations

- **Versatility and adaptability**: Nonlinear career paths demonstrate a candidate's ability to adapt to various environments and roles. This flexibility can be highly valuable in dynamic industries where versatility is crucial.
- **Diverse skill set**: Candidates with nonlinear career paths often bring a broad range of skills and perspectives. Their diverse experiences can lead to innovative problem-solving and unique contributions to the workplace.
- **Evidence of resilience**: Successfully navigating a nonlinear career path requires resilience and resourcefulness. Recruiters may view these candidates as capable of overcoming challenges and thriving in uncertain conditions.

Challenges in Recruiter Evaluations

- **Perceived lack of focus**: Nonlinear career paths can sometimes be perceived as indicating a lack of focus or commitment. Recruiters might question the candidate's long-term dedication to the role or industry.
- **Complexity in skill assessment**: Evaluating the relevance of a diverse skill set can be challenging. Recruiters may struggle to map the candidate's varied experiences to the specific requirements of the role.
- **Bias toward traditional pathways**: There is often an inherent bias in favor of traditional, linear career paths. Recruiters may undervalue the unique strengths of nonlinear candidates due to preconceived notions about career success and stability.

Comparative Analysis

Recruitment Strategies

To effectively evaluate candidates from both career pathways, recruiters must employ different strategies:

- **Competency-based assessment**: For nonlinear candidates, recruiters can focus on competencies rather than job titles. This involves identifying transferable skills and experiences that align with the job's requirements.
- **Narrative resumes and interviews**: Encouraging nonlinear candidates to provide narrative resumes or detailed explanations of their career journey can help recruiters understand the context and relevance of their diverse experiences.
- **Behavioral and situational interviews**: These interview techniques can help assess how candidates from both types of pathways have applied their skills in various scenarios, providing a more holistic view of their capabilities.

Organizational Fit

- **Culture and values alignment**: Assessing how well candidates align with the company's culture and values is essential. Nonlinear candidates might bring fresh perspectives that align well with innovative or entrepreneurial cultures, while linear candidates might fit better in traditional, hierarchical organizations.
- **Team dynamics**: Understanding how candidates will integrate into existing teams is important. Nonlinear candidates can introduce diversity of thought, which can be beneficial for team creativity and problem-solving, whereas linear candidates might ensure consistency and stability.

Working with Recruiters

Understanding Your UVP

The first step toward working effectively with recruiters is to understand, enhance, and articulate your UVP from chapter 2. Reflect on the following:

- **Skill diversity:** Nonlinear career paths often involve developing a broad range of skills. Identify the transferable skills you've gained and how they can benefit your target employers.
- **Adaptability and learning agility:** Demonstrate how your varied experiences have made you adaptable and quick to learn new things—traits highly valued in today's fast-changing work environments.
- **Innovative thinking:** Highlight instances where your diverse background allowed you to bring fresh perspectives and innovative solutions to problems.

Crafting a Cohesive Career Narrative

In chapter 4 you created a cohesive narrative that ties together your varied experiences. This is a crucial step as it helps employers see the logical progression in your career and understand how your experiences make you a strong candidate for the role. This involves:

- **Identifying a common theme:** Look for overarching themes in your career, such as problem-solving, leadership, or creativity. The common theme throughout my career is that each role I've had has enabled me to create innovative solutions to complex business challenges and given me a greater understanding of the holistic business by understanding its

parts. This theme should be evident in your resume, cover letter, and interview responses.
- **Storytelling:** Use storytelling techniques to weave your diverse roles into a compelling career story. Explain how each position has contributed to your professional growth and prepared you for the role you are targeting.
- **Highlighting achievements:** Focus on your achievements rather than job titles. Where possible, quantify your successes with metrics to demonstrate your impact and effectiveness.

Optimizing Your Resume and LinkedIn Profile

Your resume and LinkedIn profile are often the first points of contact with potential employers. By optimizing these elements, you ensure that employers quickly grasp your strengths and suitability for the role. To make a strong impression:

- **Functional or hybrid resume:** Consider using a functional or hybrid resume format. This allows you to group your skills and achievements by category rather than chronologically, emphasizing your strengths and relevant experiences.
- **Tailored content:** Tailor your resume and LinkedIn profile to each job application. Highlight the skills and experiences most relevant to the position you are applying for.
- **Professional headline and summary:** Craft a compelling headline and summary that encapsulate your UVP and career narrative.

Networking and Leveraging Connections

Networking is a powerful tool for anyone with a nonlinear career path. Invest in building a robust network; it will open doors and provide support during your career transition. To make the most of your connections, follow these tips:

- **Industry events and conferences:** Attend industry events and conferences to meet professionals in your target field. This helps you stay updated on industry trends and expand your network.
- **Informational interviews:** Conduct informational interviews with individuals in roles or industries you are interested in. This can provide valuable insights and potentially lead to job opportunities.
- **Leverage LinkedIn:** Use LinkedIn to connect with industry professionals, join relevant groups, and participate in discussions. Focus on recommendations over endorsements from colleagues. They hold more weight and add credibility to your profile.

Showcasing Continuous Learning and Development

Demonstrating a commitment to continuous learning is essential, especially when transitioning between different fields and roles. Continuous learning shows employers that you are dedicated to staying current and improving your skill set. Consider:

- **Online courses and certifications:** Enroll in online courses and certifications relevant to your target industry. Platforms like Coursera, Udemy, and LinkedIn Learning offer a wide range of options.
- **Professional development workshops:** Attend workshops and seminars to stay updated on industry trends and enhance your skills.
- **Personal projects and volunteering:** Engage in personal projects or volunteer work that aligns with your career goals. These can provide practical experience and demonstrate your proactive approach to learning.

Preparing for Interviews

Effective interview preparation is key to making a strong impression. It will help you present yourself as a confident and capable candidate. Focus on:

- **Crafting your narrative:** Be ready to articulate your career story clearly and confidently. Practice explaining how your diverse experiences have prepared you for the role.
- **Addressing concerns:** Anticipate questions about your nonlinear path and prepare thoughtful responses. Emphasize how your varied background equips you with unique insights and problem-solving abilities.
- **Behavioral questions:** Prepare for behavioral interview questions by using the STAR method. Highlight how you've successfully navigated challenges in different roles.

Leveraging Soft Skills

Soft skills are often honed through diverse experiences and are highly valued by employers. These skills are crucial in nearly any role and can set you apart from other candidates. Highlight skills such as:

- **Communication:** Demonstrate your ability to communicate effectively across different contexts and audiences.
- **Collaboration:** Showcase your experience working with diverse teams and adapting to different work environments.
- **Problem-solving:** Provide examples of how your varied experiences have enhanced your problem-solving capabilities.

Seeking Professional Guidance

Finally, consider seeking guidance from career coaches or mentors. Professional guidance can provide clarity and confidence during your career transition. They can provide:

- **Personalized advice:** Offer tailored advice on how to position yourself based on your unique background and career goals.
- **Resume and interview coaching:** Help refine your resume, LinkedIn profile, and interview skills to better align with employer expectations.
- **Industry insights:** Share valuable insights into your target industry and potential career paths.

Positioning yourself effectively to future employers when you have a nonlinear career path requires a strategic approach. By understanding your UVP, crafting a cohesive career narrative, optimizing your resume and LinkedIn profile, networking, showcasing continuous learning, preparing thoroughly for interviews, leveraging soft skills, and seeking professional guidance, you can turn your diverse experiences into a compelling advantage. Embrace your unique journey and use it to demonstrate the breadth and depth of your skills, adaptability, and innovative thinking. With the right approach, you can position yourself as a valuable asset to any organization.

CONCLUSION

EMBRACING YOUR NONLINEAR CAREER PATH

As you reach the end of this journey, you need to reflect on the major themes and key takeaways this book has explored. Whether you are just beginning to navigate your career or are at a crossroads, the concepts discussed here are meant to empower you to embrace your unique path and use it as a strength in achieving your professional and personal goals.

Major Themes

- **Creating space for self-discovery:** The importance of introspection and creating mental and emotional space to explore what truly drives you is a foundational theme of this book. Before you can map out your career, you must understand your passions, values, and the core elements that make you unique.
- **Understanding and articulating your why:** Finding your purpose, or your why, is critical to aligning your career choices with your personal goals. The frameworks provided, such as the Finding Your Why framework, guide you through

self-reflection to identify the key drivers behind your most fulfilling experiences.
- **The power of a nonlinear path:** Nonlinear careers are often seen as unconventional, but this book argues that they offer a diverse skill set and a rich tapestry of experiences. The versatility and adaptability that come with such a path are valuable assets, providing a broad perspective that can be leveraged in various roles.
- **Crafting a cohesive career narrative:** A key strategy discussed is the importance of weaving your varied experiences into a cohesive career narrative. By doing so, you can clearly articulate your journey, making it easier for potential employers or partners to understand how your diverse background uniquely qualifies you for new opportunities.
- **Owning your UVP:** The idea of owning your career journey—embracing every role, challenge, and accomplishment as part of your personal and professional development—is a central theme. This book provides tools for defining and owning your UVP, enabling you to confidently present yourself in any professional setting.

Key Takeaways

- **Self-reflection is nonnegotiable:** Your career decisions should stem from a deep understanding of yourself. Regular self-reflection is necessary to stay aligned with your evolving goals and values.
- **Embrace flexibility and adaptability:** A nonlinear path should not be seen as a disadvantage. Instead, view it as a source of strength that equips you with a wide range of skills and the ability to adapt to different challenges.
- **Leverage your unique narrative:** Your career narrative is a powerful tool. Use it to connect the dots of your experiences

in a way that highlights your growth, skills, and readiness for the next step in your career.
- **Continuous learning is essential:** Whether through formal education, on-the-job experiences, or self-directed learning, continuous development is key to staying relevant and advancing in your career.
- **Own your journey:** Confidence in your unique career path will set you apart. By owning your story and presenting it authentically, you demonstrate resilience, creativity, and a commitment to your personal and professional growth.

I hope this book encourages you to see your career as a journey that is uniquely yours. It's not about following a predetermined path but about creating your own, guided by self-awareness, purpose, and the courage to embrace your nonlinear trajectory. Your career, like life itself, is a mosaic of experiences—with each piece adding depth and richness to the bigger picture. As you move forward, remember to celebrate your journey, stay open to new opportunities, and continue to grow into the professional you aspire to be.

URGENT PLEA!

Thank You For Reading My Book!
I really appreciate all of your feedback and
I love hearing what you have to say.

I need your input to make the next version of this
book and my future books better.

Please take two minutes now to leave a helpful review on
Amazon letting me know what you thought of the book.
Thanks so much!
- **Kristin Jemison**

Made in United States
North Haven, CT
21 March 2025

67049892R00075